Mini Instant Pot Cookbook

The Complete Guide of Mini Instant Pot for Beginners With Mouth-Watering And Easy-to-Make Recipes for Your Everyday Cooking

By Erica Jones

TABLE OF CONTENTS

INTRODUCTION

Most people today do not have the time (or energy) to cook food at home.

Instead, they rely on fast food and instant food products. Unfortunately, despite the convenience these options provide, they are not what you can call "healthy".

In fact, fast food has been linked to numerous health problems, as reported in scientific research (https://www.ncbi.nlm.nih.gov/pmc/articles/PMC4598125/). Regular consumption of foods that are high in fat, grease, sugar, salt and additives can shoot up the risk of ailments including heart disease, diabetes, kidney problems, and high blood pressure, among many others.

It's for this reason that health experts and medical practitioners are encouraging people to cook their meals at home, and use high quality and healthy ingredients.

If you're one of those people who are too busy to cook meals at home, here's the solution for you: the Mini Instant Pot. It's like the Instant Pot but smaller in size. It is just as versatile and convenient as its bigger counterpart.

This book is a comprehensive guide on how to use the Mini Instant Pot. In this book, you're going to find the basic details on how to use this multi-cooker, and how to take good care of it. You will also see 70 delicious, healthy and easy-to-prepare recipes that you can cook using this popular kitchen device.

For sure, you're going to have so much fun using this book! So are you ready to get started?

CHAPTER 1: WHY CHOOSE MINI INSTANT POT?

Before we get to the exciting part—which is cooking delicious and enticing recipes, let's first get to know more about the Mini Instant Pot and what it can do for you.

WHAT IS EXACTLY A MINI INSTANT POT (3-QUART)?

The Mini Instant Pot, also known as the Instant Pot Duo Mini, is a smaller version of the Instant Pot. It is also a multi-cooker that serves the purpose of seven kitchen appliances, which include the following:

- Rice Cooker
- Pressure Cooker
- Slow Cooker
- Sauté Pan
- Yogurt Maker
- Food Warmer
- Steamer

If the Instant Pot is too big for you, this is the perfect device for you to use. It is ideal for couples or small families, or people who live alone in the house. It's also the perfect travel companion that you can easily bring when you go on a trip in your RV or boat.

But don't think that because it's tiny, you won't be able to cook enough food. In fact, it can cook up to 6 cups of rice!

Its dimensions are 7.8 x 5 inches (19.8 x 12.7 centimeters).

The Mini Instant Pot comes with the following:

- Stainless steel inner cooking pot with no chemical coating and is of food grade 304
- Measuring cup for rice
- Rice paddle
- Soup spoon
- Stainless steel steamer rack without handles
- Condensation collector
- Detachable Power Cord
- User Manual
- Reference Guide
- Recipe Booklet

Make sure that the parts are complete when you buy your Mini Instant Pot.

ADVANTAGES OF USING MINI INSTANT POT

There are many advantages to using this smaller version of the Instant Pot. People who buy this kitchen appliance have many good things to say about it. If you browse the web, you can find and read many positive reviews about this multi-cooker as well.

Here are some of the benefits of using the Mini Instant Pot:

1 – CONVENIENCE

Like the Instant Pot, the Mini Instant Pot also provides users with utmost convenience for cooking and preparing meals.

For one, you can use it for seven cooking functions. It means that you don't need a separate pan for sautéing your vegetables and another appliance for pressure cooking your meat. You can do this both using the Mini Instant Pot.

This also means fewer pots and pans to wash, saving you both time and energy. And this device is also so easy to clean that you'll find yourself spending less and less time in the kitchen to get the work done.

2 – USER FRIENDLINESS

People who use both the Instant Pot and Mini Instant Pot say that the latter is more user-friendly. There are several reasons for this.

One is that this device has fewer buttons. For example, if you'd like to make yogurt, you only need to press one button. No more confusion with the time adjustments and so on.

And you can now switch between less, normal and more heat during the sautéing process without having to turn off the pot first.

Plus, all the preset buttons now have low, normal and high preset times.

Moreover, this appliance comes with a one-touch button operation, which recalls the previous customized cooking function that you used. So if you're going to make the same recipe again, you can simply press one button and that's it! The device will do the cooking for you. How easy is that?

3 – CHEAPER COST

Then there's also the fact that the Mini Instant Pot is cheaper than the regular Instant Pot because it's smaller in size. You can get it for only $50!

This is a good kitchen appliance to invest in, and because it comes at an affordable price, you can easily save money to buy this for your home.

4 – PRESERVATION OF FLAVOR AND NUTRIENTS

Because the device cooks the food in a fully sealed compartment, all the flavors, aroma, and of course, the nutrients are retained within the food. This is why, dishes cooked using this device are much healthier compared to those cooked using regular pots and pans.

WHERE TO BUY MINI INSTANT POT

There are various places where you can buy your Mini Instant Pot. You can purchase one from your local appliance store, or if you prefer to shop online, here are some links you can consider:

- Instant Pot Official Website (https://store.instantpot.com/products/duo-mini-3-quart)
- Amazon.com (https://www.amazon.com/Instant-Pot-Duo-Mini-Programmable/dp/B06Y1YD5W7)
- eBay.com (https://www.ebay.com/p/Instant-Pot-Duo-Mini-Electric-Pressure-Cooker-Black/11019365076)
- Walmart.com (https://www.walmart.com/browse/home/instant-pot/4044_90548_90546_7523641)
- Target.com (https://www.target.com/p/instant-pot-duo-mini-3qt-pressure-cooker/-/A-52460579)

You can also check out this link (https://instantpot.com/where-to-buy/) to find place where you can buy this kitchen appliance.

HOW TO CHOOSE A PERFECT MINI INSTANT POT

Just like when you're buying any other kitchen appliance, you need to exercise due diligence when shopping for the Mini Instant Pot. Although it only comes in one size, there are still other things that you have to look into before making the final decision to buy. Here are some tips that will help you find the perfect Mini Instant Pot.

- **Shop around.** The links provided above are just few of the many places where you can buy your Mini Instant Pot. However, you need to make sure that the online shop you choose to buy from is reputable and safe. You don't want sending your money and not getting what you paid for. Plus, you also need to compare the prices including the shipping cost and any other hidden charges. Some online shops sell the device for a much cheaper price but would charge high costs on shipping and so on.
- **Read online reviews.** Look for reviews written by people who have actually tried using this device, and those who purchased it from the online shop where you plan to buy it. This way, you can learn from other people's experiences. This will help you make an informed buying decision.
- **Check the policies for refunds and returns.** If there is any damage to the Mini Instant Pot, you would need to return it and ask for refund. But to make sure that you will get your money back, read the policies first before placing your order and sending your payment.

So far, you've gotten to know about the basic details of the Mini Instant Pot. But there are still more that you should know about such as the buttons and features, different cooking methods, its difference from the regular Instant Pot and so on. We'll talk about all these and more in the next chapter.

CHAPTER 2: KNOW ABOUT ITS FEATURES AND BUTTONS

In this chapter, we will discuss the basic features of the Mini Instant Pot, and the various ways you can use it for cooking. We'll also tackle its major differences from the regular Instant Pot, just in case you're also considering buying this device.

DIFFERENT BUTTONS & FEATURES

The Mini Instant Pot features 11 "Smart Programmable" digital controls, which include the following:

1. Rice
2. Sauté
3. Steam
4. Pressure Cook (Manual)
5. Slow Cook
6. Soup/Broth
7. Meat/Stew
8. Bean/Chili
9. Yogurt
10. Porridge
11. Keep Warm

Each program comes with three adjustable settings:

- Less
- Normal
- More

The sauté and slow cook buttons have three temperatures:

- High
- Normal
- Low

The device also comes with a 24-hour delay start that lets you postpone the cooking until you're ready to have your dinner. It also has an automatic "keep warm" feature which retains the heat in the food until it's ready to serve.

DIFFERENT COOKING METHODS

Thanks to the Mini Instant Pot, you can now use only one device to use several cooking methods.

- **Sauté** – Sautéing is a type of cooking method which cooks food over small amount of oil or fat over high heat. This is commonly used for browning meat and poultry, and searing vegetables. The term "sauté" comes from the French word "sauter", which means "jump". The sauté button in the Mini Instant Pot is also sometimes used to boil, simmer and reduce liquid.

- **Steam** – Steaming is the process of cooking food using boiling water that vaporizes into steam. The heat is carried to the food, which is usually placed above the boiling water. The food does not have contact with the water, which results in a more intense flavor and at the same time, nutrient preservation.
- **Pressure Cook** – In this cooking method, water or other cooking liquid is placed inside a sealed pot. The pot either a pressure cooker or an Instant Pot produces internal pressure and high temperature which cooks the food more quickly.
- **Slow Cook** – This one involves simmering food in low heat for long periods, resulting in flavorful dishes and soft meat or vegetables.

The other buttons in the Mini Instant Pot are used for cooking specific types of food:

- Soups or broth
- Meat
- Beans and chili
- Yogurt
- Rice
- Porridge

NORMAL INSTANT POT VS. MINI INSTANT POT

If you're like most people, you're probably wondering what the difference between a regular Instant Pot and the Mini Instant Pot is.

The most obvious difference is the size. The regular Instant Pot is six to eight quarts while the mini version is only three quarts. If you're cooking only for two to four people, the smaller pot is of course, the better option. It takes up less space in the kitchen counter, and it is more portable if you want to take it somewhere else. The small size definitely spells convenience.

But you also have to know that the Mini Instant Pot does not have some of the buttons of the regular Instant Pot Duo. It does not have the preset buttons for egg, poultry, cake and multi-grain. But this doesn't mean you can no longer cook rice, bake cake or cook chicken. You can use the other cooking methods for these foods.

Chapter 3: Amazing Tips & Cautions of Using Mini Instant Pot

You've already learned a great deal about the Mini Instant Pot, but wait, there's a lot more! In this chapter, you will find amazing tips as well as cautions for using this device so you can use it properly and safely.

Tips of Using Mini Instant Pot

Even with its small size, the Mini Instant Pot may still appear intimidating to any beginner. That's because it has plenty buttons and features. But as what you've read in the previous chapter, the device is not complicated at all. Plus, we will provide you with these tips that will make it easier for you to make use of your Mini Instant Pot.

Tip # 1 – Perform the water test

What is the water test? This is the recommended test by the manufacturers of the Instant Pot. It entails boiling water to break in the device. This is in fact a great way to familiarize yourself with the functions of the device. It will teach you how to seal the pot, how the pressure builds up, and how to use the pressure release.

Tip # 2 – Use the right amount of liquid

Always use the amount of liquid recommended in the recipe that you're using. Remember that you need enough liquid for the Mini Instant Pot to come to pressure. If you don't use the right amount of liquid, the food will not be cooked evenly or properly.

Tip # 3 – Use appropriate accessories

Only use accessories that come with the Mini Instant Pot. Or if recommended in the recipe you're using, then make sure that it's made of suitable materials that won't melt or burn inside the pot during cooking.

Tip # 4 – Use the Keep Warm and Delay Start Features

These features have been added to the Mini Instant Pot for your convenience. Take advantage of these. The "delay start" ensures that the food is cooked just in time for dinner while the "keep warm" keeps the food warm until it is ready to be served. As you will later on find out, both of these will make cooking easier for you.

Tip # 5 – Preheat your liquid

If you'd like to reduce the cooking time even more, what you can do is to heat the sauce first in the Mini Instant Pot by using the sauté mode. You don't have to seal the pot. You can even add the meat into the sauce and let it simmer for a few minutes before pressure cooking.

Tip # 6 – Brown the meat first

A great way to come up with more flavorful dishes is by browning the meat or poultry first before pressure cooking. This is also done using the sauté mode. Basically, you will have to cook the meat or poultry first in oil before sealing the pot and cooking with pressure.

Tip # 7 - Deglaze

You'll find that many recipes require deglazing. Do not skip this part even when you're in a rush. After you're done sautéing your meat or chicken, you can deglaze the pot using liquid (water, stock, broth or even wine), and then scrape the bottom part of the pot with a wooden spoon to take out the brown bits and incorporate this into the cooking liquid. This adds more flavor to the dish.

Tip # 8 – Use the Saut Button to Reduce Liquid

If you're done pressure cooking and there's still a lot of liquid, or you haven't achieved the desired consistency, you can simmer the liquid by using the sauté button. And then you just wait for the liquid to be reduced to half.

Tip # 9 – Add Flour or Corn Starch After Pressure Cooking

Some people make the mistake of adding the thickener before pressure cooking. But this will only result in lumpy texture that you certainly do not want. What you should do is to add the flour or corn starch after you're done pressure cooking.

Tip # 10 – Always Follow the Instructions

Read the manual that comes with the device and follow all the instructions carefully. Same is true when using recipes.

Cautions You Must Know

It's important to use the Mini Instant Pot with extra precaution. Like any pressure cooker, it can cause damage or injury if you make a mistake in using it. Below, you'll find some of the cautions that you must keep in mind:

Safety Tip # 1 – Fill the Mini Instant Pot the Right Way

Do not overcrowd your cooker or put too much liquid. The amount of food and liquid should not exceed the two-thirds line inside the pot. Be extra careful with foods that expand such as rice, pasta, beans and dried veggies. As much as possible, fill the inner pot up to half only, and add at least 1 cup of liquid to make sure the pot comes to pressure.

Safety Tip # 2 – Seal the Pot Properly

Before starting with the pressure cooking, make sure that you seal the pot properly. The lid must be placed and locked the right way. If not, the pot may explode and cause burns and injuries. Make it a point to double check that the sealing ring is in proper position under the lid and that it's clean and free of debris. If not, the lid may not lock in place. Moreover, the lid should be twisted clockwise and aligned with the arrow. If it is not correctly sealed, it will flash "lid".

Safety Tip # 3 – Do Not Open the Pot Before It Is Done Depressurizing

While the Mini Instant Pot is pressure cooking, you should never open it. No matter how tempted you are to take a peek on what's happening with your food inside, do not uncover the pot. If you do, the pot will explode, even if it's just a tiny or quick peek.

Also, after releasing the pressure, let the pot sit for a few minutes before opening the pot just to be sure. If the float valve is still up or if you're finding it hard to open the lid, this means that there's still pressure inside.

Safety Tip # 4 – Stay away from the steam

This is a common advice not only to Instant Pot users but to all those use pressure cookers. Even though the modern pressure cooker is safer and more high tech, you should still not expose any of your body parts on top of the steam valve. If you do, you're most likely to sustain a burn.

Safety Tip # 5 – Keep the pot out of children's reach

Place the Mini Instant Pot in an area in your kitchen that cannot be reached. Even the cord should not be within children's reach so there's no tendency to pull it accidentally.

Keep these tips in mind to make sure that you have a safe and worthwhile experience using your Mini Instant Pot.

CHAPTER 4: MAINTENANCE OF MINI INSTANT POT AND FAQs

Just one last chapter before the cooking part!
In this chapter, you'll learn how to take good care of your Mini Instant Pot so that it lasts a long time with you.

HOW TO CLEAN IT STEP-BY-STEP

Here's a quick step-by-step procedure on how to clean your Mini Instant Pot:

STEP # 1 – CLEAN THE EXTERIOR HOUSING AND THE RIM

Get a clean damp cloth. Use it to wipe any food debris or stain on the pot's exterior housing. It's a good idea to use a cloth made of microfiber as this takes out the dirt more easily. For the rim, remove stubborn dirt using a foam brush dipped with warm soapy water. If you don't have a foam brush, what you can do is to wrap a microfiber cloth around a stick and use this to clean the rim.

STEP # 2 – CLEAN THE INNER POT

It's good to know that the stainless steel inner pot is dishwasher safe. But you can also wash it with warm soapy water if you don't have a dishwasher. If there are any stains, you can remove this with white vinegar. For stains that cannot be removed by vinegar, try using Bar Keepers Friend, which is effective for removing hard water stains and rusts on stainless steel materials.

STEP # 3 – WASH THE LID AND THE OTHER PARTS

Wash the cover of the pot using warm soapy water. This is easy to rinse under tap water. Do not put the lid in the dishwasher. From time to time, you can clean out the other parts of the Mini Instant Pot, which includes:

- **Anti-block shield** – Push it on the side and lift it up to see if there are any food or liquid residue. Rinse and dry it. Press down to put it back to its original position.
- **Steam Release Valve** – Remove the valve and wash while pulling it up.
- **Condensation Collector** – Slide it out, take out any liquid and rinse.

STEP # 4 – CLEAN THE SEALING RING

Take note the sealing ring directly affects the process of pressure cooking so you need to take good care of it. It's a good thing that it is dishwasher safe. However, it's best to wash it by hand so that it won't be deformed or stretched easily. You only need to rinse the sealing ring unless there's stubborn food debris or stain. To get rid of stains and odor, soak in white vinegar for a few minutes. Then rinse with water.

QUICK CLEANING GUIDE & TIPS

The parts of the Mini Instant Pot that are dishwasher safe include:

- Stainless steel inner pot
- Sealing ring
- Steamer rack

Wash only periodically:

- Anti-block shield
- Steam release valve
- Condensation collector

TAKE NOTE OF MAINTENANCE TIPS

- Do not immerse the exterior housing in water or any liquid.
- Always wash the inner pot every after use.
- Wipe off food debris before it hardens and becomes difficult to remove.
- Do not use cleaning solutions with harsh chemicals. Water or soapy water will do.

So that's it! You now know how to use and take care of your Mini Instant Pot. Are you ready to get started with cooking?

CHAPTER 5: EASY BREAKFAST (10)

BOILED EGGS
Servings: 2
Preparation & Cooking Time: 10 minutes

Ingredients
- 2 cups water
- 2 eggs
- Salt and pepper to taste

Instructions
1. Add the water to the Mini Instant Pot.
2. Place a steamer rack inside.
3. Put the eggs on the rack.
4. Lock the lid in place.
5. Press the manual setting.
6. Cook at high pressure for 2 minutes.
7. Release the pressure naturally.
8. Remove the eggs and place in a bowl of cold water.

9. Let sit for 5 minutes before peeling and serving.
10. Season with the salt and pepper.

Nutritional Information per Serving

Calories 63
Total Fat 4.4 g
Saturated Fat 1.4 g
Cholesterol 164 mg
Total Carbs 0.4 g
Sugars 0.3 g
Fiber 0 g
Sodium 69 mg
Potassium 62 mg
Protein 5.6 g

STEEL CUT OATMEAL

Servings: 1
Preparation & Cooking Time: 30 minutes

Ingredients
- Cooking spray
- ¾ cup water
- ¼ cup steel cut oats
- Milk
- Honey

Instructions
1. Spray the Mini Instant Pot with oil.
2. Pour in the water.
3. Add the oats and stir.
4. Seal the pot.
5. Set it to manual.
6. Cook at high pressure for 10 minutes.
7. Release the pressure naturally.
8. Stir in the milk and honey, and the let cool for 5 minutes before serving.

Nutritional Information per Serving
Calories 164
Total Fat 3.2 g
Saturated Fat 1.6 g
Cholesterol 10 mg
Total Carbs 30.2 g
Sugars 22.9 g
Fiber 1.1 g
Sodium 59 mg
Potassium 118 mg
Protein 5.4 g

BREAKFAST BURRITO BOWL

Servings: 2-4

Preparation & Cooking Time: 30 minutes

Ingredients

- 4 eggs
- 2 tbsp. butter, melted
- Salt and pepper to taste
- ¼ lb. cooked breakfast sausage
- ¼ cup cheddar cheese, shredded
- ¼ cup avocado cubes
- ¼ cup sour cream
- ¼ cup salsa
- Chopped green onion

Instructions

1. In a bowl, beat the eggs and then whisk in the butter, salt and pepper.
2. Press the sauté setting in the Mini Instant Pot.
3. Add the egg mixture.
4. Cook for 5 minutes, stirring frequently.
5. Add the cheese and breakfast sausage.
6. Cook for 5 more minutes.
7. Transfer the mixture into serving bowls.
8. Top with the avocado, sour cream and salsa.
9. Garnish with the green onion.
10. Chill for 15 minutes before serving.

Nutritional Information per Serving

Calories 275
Total Fat 23.6 g
Saturated Fat 11 g
Cholesterol 217mg
Total Carbs 2.4 g
Sugars 1 g
Fiber 0.4 g
Sodium 464 mg
Potassium 231 mg
Protein 13.6 g

EGG WITH KALE & CHICKEN SAUSAGE MUFFINS

Servings: 2
Preparation & Cooking Time: 20 minutes

Ingredients

- 3 tsp. olive oil
- 4 oz. chicken sausage, cooked and diced
- 4 kale leaves, chopped
- Salt and pepper to taste
- 4 eggs
- ¼ cup coconut milk
- 4 tbsp. Swiss cheese, shredded
- 1 cup water

Instructions

1. Grease the insides of the Mini Instant Pot and muffin cups or mason jars.
2. Set the pot to sauté.
3. Add the chicken sausage.
4. Cook for 2 minutes.
5. Add the kale.
6. Season with the salt and pepper.
7. Cook for 3 minutes.
8. In a bowl, beat the eggs and coconut milk.
9. Sprinkle with salt and pepper.
10. Pour the sausage mixture into the muffin cups.
11. Pour the egg mixture on top.
12. Top with cheese.
13. Cover loosely with foil.
14. Pour the water into the pot.
15. Place a steamer rack inside.
16. Place one muffin cup inside.
17. Seal the pot.
18. Set it to manual.
19. Cook at high pressure for 5 minutes.
20. Release the pressure naturally.
21. Do the same steps for the other muffin cups.

Nutritional Information per Serving

Calories 343
Total Fat 25.3 g
Saturated Fat 10.3 g
Cholesterol 271 mg
Total Carbs 10.1 g
Sugars 2.5 g
Fiber 0.6 g
Sodium 953 mg
Potassium 393 mg
Protein 19.6 g

APPLE PORRIDGE

Servings: 2
Preparation & Cooking Time: 30 minutes

Ingredients

- ½ butternut squash, sliced into cubes
- 2 apples, sliced into smaller pieces
- ½ cup water
- 1/8 tsp. ginger, grated
- 1/8 tsp. cloves
- ¼ tsp. cinnamon
- 1 tbsp. maple syrup
- 1 tbsp. gelatin
- Salt to taste

Instructions

1. Add the butternut squash and apples inside the pot.
2. Add the water, ginger, cloves and cinnamon.
3. Seal the pot.
4. Set it to manual.
5. Cook at high pressure for 8 minutes.
6. Release the pressure naturally.
7. Transfer the contents to a food processor.
8. Add the maple syrup, gelatin and salt.
9. Pulse until smooth.
10. Serve either warm or cold.

Nutritional Information per Serving

Calories 333
Total Fat 0.9 g
Saturated Fat 0.1 g
Cholesterol 0 mg
Total Carbs 87 g
Sugars 38.4 g
Fiber 14 g
Sodium 99 mg
Potassium 1742 mg
Protein 4.8 g

CHOCO VANILLA OATMEAL WITH CHERRIES

Servings: 4
Preparation & Cooking Time: 30 minutes

Ingredients

- 1 tsp. butter
- 3 cups water
- 1 cup steel cut oats
- ¼ tsp. grated nutmeg
- Salt to taste
- ½ tsp. vanilla extract
- 2 tbsp. maple syrup
- 1 tbsp. brown sugar
- 1 cup fresh cherries, pitted and sliced in half
- ½ cup dark chocolate chips

Instructions

1. Coat the bottom of the Mini Instant Pot with butter.
2. Pour in the water.
3. Stir in the oats, nutmeg and salt.
4. Close the pot.
5. Set it to manual mode.
6. Cook at high pressure for 15 minutes.
7. Release the pressure naturally.
8. Stir in the vanilla and maple syrup.
9. Add the brown sugar.
10. Top with the cherries and chocolate chips.

Nutritional Information per Serving

Calories 193
Total Fat 6.4 g
Saturated Fat 3.4 g
Cholesterol 3 mg
Total Carbs 32.9 g
Sugars 16.4 g
Fiber 2.1 g
Sodium 54 mg
Potassium 101 mg
Protein 3.7 g

FRENCH TOAST CASSEROLE

Servings: 2
Preparation & Cooking Time: 50 minutes

Ingredients

- 1 egg
- ½ cup milk
- ¼ tsp. almond extract
- ¼ tsp. cinnamon
- 1/8 cup brown sugar
- 2 French breads, sliced into smaller pieces
- ½ cup fresh blueberries
- Cooking Spray
- ¾ cup water
- Slivered almonds

Instructions

1. In a bowl, beat the egg.
2. Stir in the milk, almond extract, cinnamon and brown sugar.
3. Add the bread cubes and blueberries. Mix well.
4. Spray oil in a small ceramic bowl that can fit inside your Mini Instant Pot.
5. Pour the mixture into the bowl.
6. Add the water into the pot.
7. Place a steamer rack inside the pot.
8. Put the bowl on top of the rack.
9. Close the pot and set it to manual.
10. Cook at high pressure for 25 minutes.
11. Release the pressure naturally.
12. Let cool a little and top with the almonds before serving.

Nutritional Information per Serving

Calories 307
Total Fat 5 g
Saturated Fat 1.8 g
Cholesterol 87 mg
Total Carbs 53.7 g
Sugars 17 g
Fiber 2.6 g
Sodium 481 mg
Potassium 189 mg
Protein 12.6 g

BREAKFAST PUDDING

Servings: 2
Preparation & Cooking Time: 30 minutes

Ingredients

- Cooking spray
- 1 egg
- 1 tbsp. brown sugar
- 1 tbsp. orange marmalade
- 1 tsp. vanilla
- ½ cup milk
- ½ tsp. ground cinnamon, divided
- 4 slices French bread, cubed
- 1 cup water
- Banana slices
- Raisins

Instructions

1. Coat a small ceramic bowl with cooking spray.
2. In another bowl, beat the eggs and add the brown sugar, orange marmalade, vanilla, milk and half of the cinnamon.
3. Fold in the bread cubes and mix to coat evenly.
4. Pour the mixture into the first bowl.
5. Add the water into the Mini Instant Pot.
6. Place a steamer rack inside and put the bowl on top.
7. Close the pot.
8. Set it to manual.
9. Cook at high pressure for 15 minutes.
10. Top with the banana slices and raisins before serving.

Nutritional Information per Serving

Calories 348
Total Fat 4.7 g
Saturated Fat 1.8 g
Cholesterol 87 mg
Total Carbs 64.7 g
Sugars 24.7 g
Fiber 2.8 g
Sodium 488 mg
Potassium 313 mg
Protein 12.9 g

OATMEAL WITH PEACHES

Servings: 4
Preparation & Cooking Time: 15 minutes

Ingredients

- 2 cups water
- 2 cups rolled oats
- 1 tsp. vanilla
- 1 peach, chopped
- Milk
- Maple syrup
- ½ cup almonds chopped

Instructions

1. Pour the water into the Mini Instant Pot.
2. Add the oats, vanilla and peaches.
3. Choose the porridge setting.
4. Set the time to 3 minutes.
5. Release the pressure naturally.
6. Pour the contents of the pot into bowls.
7. Stir in milk and maple syrup, and top with the almonds before serving.

Nutritional Information per Serving

Calories 239
Total Fat 5.9 g
Saturated Fat 1.3 g
Cholesterol 5 mg
Total Carbs 38.4 g
Sugars 9.9 g
Fiber 5.2 g
Sodium 32 mg
Potassium 266 mg
Protein 8.5 g

CINNAMON OATMEAL

Servings: 4
Preparation & Cooking Time: 20 minutes

Ingredients

- 3 tbsp. butter
- 1 cup steel cut oats
- 1 tsp. cinnamon
- 2 ½ cups water
- 1 tbsp. brown sugar
- 1 apple, chopped
- Salt to taste

Instructions

1. Choose the sauté setting in the Mini Instant Pot.
2. Add the butter and let it melt.
3. Add the oats, stirring frequently.
4. Cook for 2 minutes.
5. Pour in the water and add the rest of the ingredients.
6. Seal the pot.
7. Select manual function.
8. Cook at high pressure for 7 minutes.
9. Release the pressure naturally.
10. Sprinkle with a little more sugar before serving.

Nutritional Information per Serving

Calories 193
Total Fat 10.1 g
Saturated Fat 5.7 g
Cholesterol 23 mg
Total Carbs 24.2 g
Sugars 8.2 g
Fiber 3.7 g
Sodium 107 mg
Potassium 143 mg
Protein 3 g

CHAPTER 6: HEALTHY RICE & BEANS & GRAINS RECIPES (10)

JERK THIGHS WITH RICE

Servings: 2
Preparation & Cooking Time: 20 minutes

Ingredients
- 2 tsp. olive oil
- ½ onion, diced
- 1 clove garlic, minced
- 1 tbsp. Jamaican jerk seasoning
- 1 cup reduced sodium chicken broth
- ¾ cup rice, rinsed and drained
- 2 chicken thighs (boneless, skinless), sliced into cubes

Instructions
1. Set the Mini Instant Pot to sauté.
2. Pour in the olive oil.

3. Add the onion and cook for 2 to 3 minutes.
4. Add the garlic and cook for 30 seconds.
5. Sprinkle with the Jamaican jerk seasoning.
6. Pour in the chicken broth.
7. Simmer.
8. Stir in the rice.
9. Lay the chicken on top of the rice.
10. Seal the pot.
11. Choose manual mode.
12. Cook at high pressure for 7 minutes.
13. Let sit for 5 minutes.
14. Release the pressure naturally.

Nutritional Information per Serving

Calories 448
Total Fat 10.4 g
Saturated Fat 2.2 g
Cholesterol 62 mg
Total Carbs 59 g
Sugars 1.5 g
Fiber 1.5g
Sodium 405 mg
Potassium 398 mg
Protein 27.2 g

SPICED COCONUT CHICKEN & RICE

Servings: 4
Preparation & Cooking Time: 30 minutes

Ingredients

- 1 tbsp. olive oil
- 1 ginger, chopped
- 1 onion, sliced
- 3 cloves garlic, minced
- 1 tsp. ground turmeric
- ¼ tbsp. curry powder
- 2 chicken thighs
- Salt and pepper to taste
- ¼ cup water
- 1 cup coconut milk
- 1 tsp. sugar
- Cilantro leaves
- 4 cups cooked rice

Instructions

1. Choose the sauté function in the Mini Instant Pot.
2. Add the olive oil.
3. Cook the ginger and onion for 2 minutes.
4. Add the garlic, turmeric and curry powder.
5. Cook for 1 minute, stirring frequently.
6. Season the chicken with salt and pepper, and then add to the pot.
7. Pour in the water and coconut milk.
8. Seal the pot.
9. Press the manual button.
10. Cook at high pressure for 13 minutes.
11. Release the pressure quickly.
12. Stir in the sugar and garnish with the cilantro.
13. Serve with rice.

Nutritional Information per Serving

Calories 835
Total Fat 31 g
Saturated Fat 20 g
Cholesterol 90 mg
Total Carbs 60 g
Sugars 5 g
Fiber 7 g
Sodium 169 mg
Potassium 399 mg
Protein 31 g

VEGETABLE & CHEESE RISOTTO

Servings: 3
Preparation & Cooking Time: 35 minutes

Ingredients

- 2 tbsp. butter, sliced into cubes
- 1 tbsp. olive oil
- 1 onion, chopped
- Pinch of red pepper flakes, crushed
- Salt and pepper to taste
- 1 clove garlic, minced
- 4 oz. asparagus, trimmed and chopped
- 4 oz. Portobello mushrooms, chopped
- 1 cup Arborio rice
- 15 oz. vegetable broth
- 1 cup baby spinach
- ¼ cup peas
- ¼ cup Asiago cheese, grated
- ¼ cup Parmesan cheese, grated
- ¼ cup cheddar cheese, shredded
- 1 tsp. lemon zest
- 2 tsp. lemon juice

Instructions

1. Press the sauté function in the Mini Instant Pot.
2. Add the butter and olive oil.
3. Add the onion and red pepper flakes.
4. Season with the salt and pepper.
5. Cook for 3 minutes.
6. Add the garlic, asparagus, mushroom and rice.
7. Cook for 2 more minutes.
8. Add the broth.
9. Cover the pot.
10. Set the pressure to high and cook for 5 minutes.
11. Release the pressure quickly.
12. Stir in the remaining ingredients.
13. Season with salt and pepper.

Nutritional Information per Serving

Calories 434
Total Fat 16.9 g
Saturated Fat 7.9 g

Cholesterol 30 mg
Total Carbs 58.7 g
Sugars 3.6 g
Fiber 4.3g
Sodium 580 mg
Potassium 408 mg
Protein 11.8 g

MANGO & BLACK SESAME RICE PUDDING

Servings: 3
Preparation & Cooking Time: 15 minutes

Ingredients

- 3 cups milk
- ¼ cup sugar
- ½ cup rice, rinsed and drained
- Salt to taste
- 1 egg, beaten
- ½ tsp. vanilla extract
- ½ tbsp. black sesame paste
- ½ cup mango, diced

Instructions

1. Mix the milk, sugar, rice and salt in the Mini Instant Pot.
2. Cover the pot.
3. Set it to manual.
4. Cook at high pressure for 10 minutes.
5. Release the pressure naturally.
6. Press the sauté function.
7. Mix in the egg into the rice slowly, stirring the whole time.
8. Stir in the vanilla and black sesame paste.
9. Top with the fresh mango before serving.

Nutritional Information per Serving

Calories 337
Total Fat 6.8 g
Saturated Fat 3.5 g
Cholesterol 75 mg
Total Carbs 57.6 g
Sugars 31.7 g
Fiber 0.8 g
Sodium 188 mg
Potassium 243 mg
Protein 12.3 g

SOAKED GRAINS & BEANS

Servings: 4
Preparation & Cooking Time: 15 minutes

Ingredients

- ½ cup dry beans, soaked overnight
- 1 ½ cup vegetable broth
- ½ tsp. chicken taco seasoning
- Salt and black pepper to taste
- ½ tsp. Italian herbs
- ¼ tsp. garlic powder
- ¼ tsp. cumin
- ¼ tsp. smoked paprika
- ¼ tsp. onion powder
- ½ cup quinoa, rinsed
- ½ cup water

Instructions

1. Add all the ingredients except the quinoa and water to the Mini Instant Pot.
2. Place a steamer rack inside the pot.
3. Put the quinoa and water in a small bowl.
4. Place the bowl on top of the steamer rack.
5. Cover the pot.
6. Choose manual mode.
7. Cook at high pressure for 7 minutes.
8. Release the pressure naturally.
9. If the beans are not yet done, pressure cook for another minute or longer.
10. Press sauté to reduce liquid.

Nutritional Information per Serving

Calories 99
Total Fat 1.9 g
Saturated Fat 0.3 g
Cholesterol 0 mg
Total Carbs 15.3 g
Sugars 0.6 g
Fiber 2.1g
Sodium 289 mg
Potassium 235 mg
Protein 5.2 g

BEANS WITH GARLIC & SPICES

Servings: 4
Preparation & Cooking Time: 15 minutes

Ingredients

- 1 tbsp. vegetable oil
- 4 cloves garlic, chopped
- ½ tsp. cumin seeds
- 1 green chili, chopped
- 1 potato, cubed
- 2 cup green beans, chopped
- ¼ tsp. red chili powder
- ¼ tsp. turmeric
- 2 tsp. coriander
- Salt to taste
- 1 tsp. lemon juice

Instructions

1. Set the Mini Instant Pot to sauté.
2. Add the oil.
3. Cook the garlic for 1 minute.
4. Add the cumin seeds and chili.
5. Cook until the cumin seeds splutter.
6. Add the potatoes and green beans.
7. Season with the chili powder, turmeric, coriander and salt.
8. Close the pot and choose manual mode.
9. Cook at high pressure for 2 minutes.
10. Release the pressure naturally.
11. Stir in the lemon juice before serving.

Nutritional Information per Serving

Calories 89
Total Fat 3.6 g
Saturated Fat 0.7 g
Cholesterol 0 mg
Total Carbs 13.2 g
Sugars 1.4 g
Fiber 3 g
Sodium 78 mg
Potassium 320 mg
Protein 2.1 g

BLACK BEAN & MUSHROOM CHILI

Servings: 4
Preparation & Cooking Time: 30 minutes

Ingredients

- 1 cup onion, chopped
- 4 cloves garlic, minced
- 2 cups mushrooms, sliced
- 20 oz. fire roasted tomatoes
- 20 oz. black beans with liquid
- ½ tsp. oregano
- ½ tbsp. ground cumin
- ¼ tbsp. smoked paprika
- ¼ tsp. ground chipotle powder
- Salt and pepper to taste
- 8 oz. corn kernels
- Parmesan cheese

Instructions

1. Choose the sauté setting in the Mini Instant Pot.
2. Cook the onion for 5 minutes.
3. Add the garlic.
4. Cook for 1 minute.
5. Add the rest of the ingredients except the corn and Parmesan cheese.
6. Seal the pot.
7. Select manual mode.
8. Cook at high pressure for 6 minutes.
9. Release the pressure naturally.
10. Add the corn and cheese before serving.

Nutritional Information per Serving

Calories 322
Total Fat 4.8 g
Saturated Fat 0.6 g
Cholesterol 0 mg
Total Carbs 68.6 g
Sugars 14.9 g
Fiber 11.3 g
Sodium 241 mg
Potassium 1042 mg
Protein 12.8 g

HUMMUS

Servings: 4
Preparation & Cooking Time: 1 hour and 10 minutes

Ingredients

- 3 cloves garlic, crushed
- 2 cups dried chickpeas
- 4 cups water
- 1 tbsp. vegetable oil
- Salt and pepper to taste
- ½ cup olive oil, divided
- Pita bread

Instructions

1. Place the garlic and chickpeas in the Mini Instant Pot.
2. Pour in the water and oil. Stir.
3. Seal the pot.
4. Press the bean or chili function.
5. Cook for 50 minutes.
6. Release the pressure naturally.
7. Drain into a bowl.
8. Season the chickpeas with salt, pepper and 3 tablespoons olive oil.
9. Add ¼ cup of the chickpea liquid.
10. Put in a food processor.
11. Pulse until smooth.
12. Add more olive oil until smooth and desired consistency is reached.
13. Serve with pita bread.

Nutritional Information per Serving

Calories 613
Total Fat 34.7 g
Saturated Fat 4.9 g
Cholesterol 0 mg
Total Carbs 61.4 g
Sugars 10.7 g
Fiber 17.5 g
Sodium 32 mg
Potassium 887 mg
Protein 19.4 g

RISOTTO PRIMAVERA

Servings: 4
Preparation & Cooking Time: 45 minutes

Ingredients

- 2 tbsp. olive oil
- ½ cup sweet onion, chopped
- 2 tsp. fresh thyme, chopped
- 1 cup Arborio rice
- ½ cup dry white wine
- 2 cups chicken broth
- 1 cup fava beans
- 8 oz. asparagus, trimmed and chopped
- 1 cup baby spinach leaves
- ¼ cup Parmesan cheese, grated
- 1 tsp. lemon zest
- ½ tbsp. fresh lemon juice
- Salt and pepper to taste

Instructions

1. Set the Mini Instant Pot to sauté.
2. Add the oil.
3. Cook the onion for 4 minutes.
4. Add the thyme. Cook for another minute.
5. Add the rice, stirring frequently for 1 minute.
6. Pour in the wine and simmer for 1 minute.
7. Stir in the broth.
8. Seal the pot.
9. Choose manual mode.
10. Cook at high pressure for 8 minutes.
11. Release the pressure quickly.
12. Add the beans and asparagus.
13. Press the sauté mode.
14. Cook for 3 minutes.
15. Add the rest of the ingredients.
16. Turn off the Mini Instant Pot.
17. Mix well and serve.

Nutritional Information per Serving

Calories 424
Total Fat 8.7 g
Saturated Fat 1.4 g
Cholesterol 0 mg
Total Carbs 65.2 g
Sugars 4.5 g
Fiber 12.6 g
Sodium 400 mg
Potassium 752 mg
Protein 17.1 g

MUNG BEANS

Servings: 2
Preparation & Cooking Time: 50 minutes

Ingredients

- ½ cup dry mung beans
- 2 cups vegetable stock
- 2 tsp. curry powder
- Salt and pepper to taste
- ¼ tsp. garlic powder
- ½ tsp. onion powder

Instructions

1. Add all the ingredients in the Mini Instant Pot.
2. Cover the pot.
3. Choose manual mode.
4. Cook at high pressure for 25 minutes.
5. Release the pressure naturally.
6. Mash the mung beans with fork and then stir before serving.

Nutritional Information per Serving

Calories 192
Total Fat 0.9 g
Saturated Fat 0.2 g
Cholesterol 0 mg
Total Carbs 34.8 g
Sugars 4.1 g
Fiber 9.4 g
Sodium 34 mg
Potassium 686 mg
Protein 12.9 g

Chapter 7: Mouth-watering Beef, Pork & Lamb Recipes (10)

Korean Beef Bulgogi

Servings: 4
Preparation & Cooking Time: 50 minutes

Ingredients

- 1 tsp. vegetable oil
- 1 lb. lean ground beef
- 1 tbsp. pressed garlic
- ¼ cup water
- ¼ cup soy sauce
- ½ tbsp. sesame oil
- ¼ cup brown sugar
- ½ tsp. ginger powder
- Red pepper flakes
- Black pepper to taste

- Lettuce leaves
- Sesame seeds

Instructions

1. Set the Mini Instant Pot to sauté.
2. Add the oil and cook the ground beef until brown.
3. Add the garlic, water, soy sauce, sesame oil, sugar and ginger.
4. Add a pinch of red pepper flakes and pepper.
5. Stir everything.
6. Seal the pot.
7. Choose manual function.
8. Cook at high for 4 minutes.
9. Let sit for 10 minutes.
10. Release the pressure naturally.
11. Serve with lettuce and garnish with sesame seeds.

Nutritional Information per Serving

Calories 280
Total Fat 9.9 g
Saturated Fat 3.1 g
Cholesterol 101 mg
Total Carbs 10.3 g
Sugars 9.1 g
Fiber 0.2 g
Sodium 976 mg
Potassium 509 mg
Protein 35.4 g

PORK CARNITAS

Servings: 4
Preparation & Cooking Time: 50 minutes

Ingredients

- 2 tbsp. olive oil
- 1 tbsp. cumin
- 2 tsp. chili powder
- 1 tsp. oregano
- 1 tsp. paprika
- ¼ tsp. cayenne pepper
- 1 tsp. coriander powder
- Salt and pepper to taste
- 1 lb. pork shoulder, sliced into small chunks
- 1 onion, chopped
- ½ cinnamon stick
- 1 bay leaf
- 2 cloves garlic, minced
- ¼ cup orange juice
- Avocado cubes

Instructions

1. In a bowl, mix the oil, cumin, chili powder, oregano, paprika, cayenne, coriander, salt and pepper.
2. Coat all sides of the pork chunks with this mixture.
3. Choose the sauté function in the Mini Instant Pot.
4. Cook the meat until brown on all sides.
5. Remove and set aside.
6. Add the onion, cinnamon stick and bay leaf, stirring frequently.
7. Cook for 3 minutes.
8. Add the garlic, cook for 30 seconds.
9. Deglaze with the orange juice.
10. Scrape the bottom of the pot with a wooden spoon.
11. Put the meat back to the pot.
12. Cover the pot.
13. Choose manual mode.
14. Cook at high pressure for 30 minutes.
15. Release pressure naturally.
16. Serve with avocado cubes on the side.

Nutritional Information per Serving

Calories 425
Total Fat 32g
Saturated Fat 10 g
Cholesterol 102 mg
Total Carbs 6.9 g
Sugars 2.7 g
Fiber 1.8 g
Sodium 95 mg
Potassium 525 mg
Protein 27.5 g

BEEF WITH SWEET POTATO

Servings: 4
Preparation & Cooking Time: 30 minutes

Ingredients

- 1 tbsp. olive oil
- ½ lb. lean ground beef
- 1 onion, diced
- 1 clove garlic, minced
- 2 oz. diced green chili
- 2 tsp. chili powder
- 1 tsp. smoke paprika
- 1 tsp. cumin
- ¼ tsp. dried thyme
- ½ tsp. oregano
- Salt and pepper to taste
- 14 oz. tomato sauce
- 14 oz. canned diced tomatoes
- 10 oz. red kidney beans, rinsed and drained
- 1 cup sweet potato, diced
- 1 bay leaf
- ½ cup water
- Tortilla chips, crushed
- Cilantro

Instructions

1. Choose the sauté function in the Mini Instant Pot.
2. Add the olive oil.
3. Cook the ground beef until brown.
4. Add the onion and cook for 3 minutes.
5. Add the garlic and cook for 1 minute.
6. Add the green chili, spices, salt and pepper. Mix well.
7. Stir in the rest of the ingredients except the chips and cilantro.
8. Simmer for 3 minutes.
9. Cover the pot.
10. Select the manual mode.
11. Cook at high pressure for 5 minutes.
12. Release the pressure naturally.
13. Discard the bay leaf.
14. Serve with tortilla chips and cilantro.

Nutritional Information per Serving

Calories 455
Total Fat 5.1 g
Saturated Fat 1.6 g
Cholesterol 51 mg
Total Carbs 67.9 g
Sugars 13.3 g
Fiber 16.3 g
Sodium 661 mg
Potassium 2074 mg
Protein 37 g

PICADILLO

Servings: 4
Preparation & Cooking Time: 30 minutes

Ingredients

- 1 tsp. olive oil
- ¼ lb. lean ground beef
- Salt and pepper to taste
- 1 onion, chopped
- 1 clove garlic, minced
- 1 red bell pepper, chopped
- 1 tbsp. cilantro
- 1 tomato, chopped
- 1 bay leaf
- 1 tbsp. capers
- 1 tsp. ground cumin
- 1 cup tomato sauce
- 3 tbsp. water

Instructions

1. Set the Mini Instant Pot to sauté.
2. Pour in the olive oil.
3. Cook the ground beef until brown.
4. Add the onion, garlic, bell pepper, cilantro and tomato.
5. Season with the salt and pepper.
6. Add the capers with two tablespoons of its juice.
7. Add the cumin and bay leaf.
8. Pour in the tomato sauce and water.
9. Cover the pot.
10. Set it to manual.
11. Cook at high pressure for 15 minutes.
12. Release the pressure quickly.

Nutritional Information per Serving

Calories 207
Total Fat 8.5 g
Saturated Fat 5 g
Cholesterol 74 mg
Total Carbs 5 g
Sugars 3 g
Fiber 1 g
Sodium 75 mg
Potassium 353 mg
Protein 25 g

MEATBALLS

Servings: 4
Preparation & Cooking Time: 20 minutes

Ingredients

- 1 lb. lean ground beef or pork
- ¼ cup Parmesan, grated
- ¼ cup almond flour
- 2 tsp. dried parsley
- 1 egg, beaten
- ½ tsp. dried oregano
- Salt and pepper to taste
- ½ cup beef broth
- 1 cup tomato sauce

Instructions

1. Mix the ground beef or pork, Parmesan, almond flour, parsley, egg, oregano, salt and pepper.
2. Form 10 to 12 balls.
3. Pour the tomato sauce and broth into the Mini Instant Pot.
4. Add the meatballs. Cook in batch if the meatballs don't fit all at once.
5. Roll to coat with the sauce.
6. Cover the pot.
7. Choose manual setting.
8. Cook at high pressure for 9 minutes.
9. Pour the sauce over the meatballs before serving.

Nutritional Information per Serving

Calories 280
Total Fat 10.8 g
Saturated Fat 4.2 g
Cholesterol 147 mg
Total Carbs 4.3 g
Sugars 2.8 g
Fiber 1.2 g
Sodium 572 mg
Potassium 707 mg
Protein 39.9 g

BEEF & PICKLED CARROTS

Servings: 4
Preparation & Cooking Time: 35 minutes

Ingredients

- 1 tbsp. olive oil
- ¼ cup onion, sliced
- 2 cloves garlic, sliced
- 1 tbsp. ginger, minced
- ½ lb. lean ground beef
- Salt and pepper to taste
- ¼ cup chicken broth
- ¼ cup basil leaves, chopped
- 1 tbsp. lime juice
- ½ tsp. sesame oil
- ½ tbsp. soy sauce
- 1 carrot, sliced into strips
- ¼ cup vinegar
- ½ tsp. salt
- ½ tsp. sugar

Instructions

1. Select sauté in the Mini Instant Pot.
2. Add the olive oil.
3. Cook the onion, garlic and ginger for 1 minute.
4. Add the ground beef and cook for 4 minutes.
5. Break the beef to separate.
6. Season with the salt and pepper.
7. Add the chicken broth, basil, lime juice, sesame oil and soy sauce. Mix well.
8. Cover the pot.
9. Choose manual mode.
10. Cook at high pressure for 4 minutes.
11. Release the pressure naturally.
12. While waiting, mix the carrots with vinegar, salt and sugar.
13. Serve the beef with the pickled carrots.

Nutritional Information per Serving

Calories 298
Total Fat 20 g
Saturated Fat 10 g
Cholesterol 2 mg
Total Carbs 8 g
Sugars 3 g
Fiber 1 g
Sodium 57 mg
Potassium 375 mg
Protein 22 g

CORNED BEEF WITH CABBAGE

Servings: 4
Preparation & Cooking Time: 1 hour and 15 minutes

Ingredients

- 1 lb. corned beef, rinsed and dried
- 1 onion, sliced
- 2 cloves garlic, crushed
- ½ tsp. yellow mustard seeds
- ½ tsp. whole black peppercorns
- ½ tsp. coriander seeds
- ¼ tsp. allspice whole
- 2 cloves whole
- 2 bay leaves
- 2 cups water
- 1 cup cabbage, chopped

Instructions

1. Add the corned beef and the rest of the ingredients except the cabbage into the Mini Instant Pot. Mix well.
2. Close the pot.
3. Set it to manual.
4. Cook at high pressure for 50 minutes.
5. Release the pressure naturally.
6. Transfer the corned beef to a serving bowl.
7. Add the cabbage to the pot.
8. Cover and set to manual.
9. Cook at high pressure for 2 minutes.
10. Serve the corned beef with the cabbage.

Nutritional Information per Serving

Calories 213
Total Fat 14.4 g
Saturated Fat 6.1 g
Cholesterol 71 mg
Total Carbs 4.4 g
Sugars 1.8 g
Fiber 1.2 g
Sodium 1011 mg
Potassium 248 mg
Protein 15.9 g

PORK STRIPS IN GARLIC CREAM SAUCE

Servings: 2
Preparation & Cooking Time: 25 minutes

Ingredients

- 1 tbsp. butter
- 2 pork chops, sliced into strips
- Salt and pepper to taste
- 1 cup chicken broth
- 6 cloves garlic, crushed
- 1 tbsp. flour
- ¼ cup almond milk

Instructions

1. Press the sauté function in the Mini Instant Pot.
2. Add the butter.
3. Season the pork strips with salt and pepper.
4. Cook the pork strips until brown on both sides.
5. Take the pork out of the pot.
6. Pour in the chicken broth to deglaze the pot.
7. Put the pork chops back and put the garlic cloves on top.
8. Seal the pot.
9. Choose the manual setting.
10. Cook at high pressure for 8 minutes.
11. Release the pressure naturally.
12. Stir in the almond milk and flour.
13. Simmer for 3 minutes.

Nutritional Information per Serving

Calories 423
Total Fat 33.6 g
Saturated Fat 17.7 g
Cholesterol 84 mg
Total Carbs 8.1 g
Sugars 1.5 g
Fiber 1 g
Sodium 485 mg
Potassium 500 mg
Protein 22.1 g

PORK CHOP & CINNAMON APPLESAUCE

Servings: 2
Preparation & Cooking Time: 25 minutes

Ingredients

- 2 pork chops
- Salt and pepper to taste
- 1 onion, sliced
- 2 cloves garlic, minced
- 1 tsp. cinnamon
- 2 apples, sliced thinly
- ½ cup chicken broth
- 1 tbsp. honey
- 1 tbsp. soy sauce
- 1 tbsp. butter
- 1 tbsp. cornstarch mixed with 2 tbsp. water

Instructions

1. Rub the pork chops with salt and pepper.
2. Choose the sauté button in the Mini Instant Pot.
3. Add the olive oil.
4. Brown the pork chops for 3 minutes.
5. Remove from the pot and set aside.
6. Add the sliced onion and cook for 1 minute.
7. Add the garlic and cook for 30 seconds.
8. Add the cinnamon and apple slices.
9. Deglaze the pot with the broth.
10. Stir in the honey and soy sauce.
11. Put the pork back to the pot.
12. Cover the pot.
13. Select manual mode.
14. Cook at high pressure for 1 minute.
15. Release the pressure naturally.
16. Stir in the butter and cornstarch with water.
17. Simmer for 1 minute.
18. Serve warm.

Nutritional Information per Serving

Calories 494
Total Fat 26.5 g
Saturated Fat 11.2 g
Cholesterol 84 mg
Total Carbs 46.4 g
Sugars 34.5 g
Fiber 7.3 g
Sodium 743 mg
Potassium 676 mg
Protein 21.1 g

LAMB MEATBALLS WITH TOMATO SAUCE

Servings: 3
Preparation & Cooking Time: 20 minutes

Ingredients

- ½ lb. ground lamb
- 1 egg, beaten
- 1 clove garlic, minced
- ¼ cup feta cheese, crumbled
- ¼ cup breadcrumbs
- ½ tbsp. water
- 2 tbsp. parsley, chopped
- Salt and pepper to taste
- 1 tbsp. olive oil
- 1 onion, chopped
- 1 green bell pepper, chopped
- 14 oz. tomatoes
- 3 oz. tomato sauce
- ½ tsp. dried oregano

Instructions

1. In a bowl, mix the ground lamb, egg, garlic, cheese, breadcrumbs, water, parsley, salt and pepper.
2. Form into balls.
3. Select the sauté function in the Mini Instant Pot.
4. Add the oil.
5. Cook the onion and bell pepper for 2 minutes.
6. Pour in the tomatoes, tomato sauce and oregano.
7. Season with a little more salt and pepper.
8. Place the meatballs in the pot.
9. Roll to coat with the sauce.
10. Secure the pot.
11. Choose manual setting.
12. Cook at high pressure for 8 minutes.
13. Release the pressure quickly.

Nutritional Information per Serving

Calories 331
Total Fat 15.3 g
Saturated Fat 5.1 g
Cholesterol 134 mg
Total Carbs 20.9 g
Sugars 9.5 g
Fiber 4 g
Sodium 443 mg
Potassium 857 mg
Protein 28.6 g

CHAPTER 8: DELICIOUS POULTRY & SEAFOOD RECIPES (10)

ROSEMARY CHICKEN WITH POTATOES

Servings: 2
Preparation & Cooking Time: 30 minutes

Ingredients
- 1 lb. chicken breast, sliced into strips
- 3 tsp. dried rosemary
- 1 tsp. garlic powder
- Salt and pepper to taste
- 1 tbsp. olive oil
- 1 onion, sliced
- 1 potato, sliced
- ¼ cup water
- 2 tbsp. all purpose flour
- 2 tbsp. butter

Instructions

1. Season the chicken strips with garlic powder, rosemary, salt and pepper.
2. Turn on the sauté function in the Mini Instant Pot.
3. Pour in the olive oil.
4. Brown the chicken strips.
5. Remove the chicken and place on a plate.
6. Add the onion and cook for 1 minute.
7. Put the chicken back to the pot.
8. Add the potato slices and water.
9. Cover the pot.
10. Press the manual button.
11. Cook at high pressure for 12 minutes.
12. Release the pressure naturally.
13. Transfer the contents to a pot.
14. Take a tablespoon of the cooking liquid. Discard the rest.
15. Stir in the flour and butter.
16. Put the mixture to the pot.
17. Press sauté and simmer until the gravy has thickened.
18. Serve the chicken and potatoes with gravy.

Nutritional Information per Serving

Calories 547
Total Fat 24.7 g
Saturated Fat 8.5 g
Cholesterol 176 mg
Total Carbs 28.2 g
Sugars 3.4 g
Fiber 4.2 g
Sodium 207 mg
Potassium 1323 mg
Protein 51.7 g

Chicken in Coconut Milk

Servings: 4
Preparation & Cooking Time: 30 minutes

Ingredients

- 1 tsp. ginger, chopped
- 2 cloves garlic, crushed
- ¼ tsp. five spice powder
- 1 tbsp. soy sauce
- 1 tsp. fish sauce
- ½ cup coconut milk
- 2 chicken drumsticks
- Salt and pepper to taste
- 1 tsp. coconut oil
- 1 onion, chopped
- 1 tsp. lime juice
- ¼ cup fresh cilantro leaves, chopped

Instructions

1. Add the ginger, garlic, five spice, soy sauce and fish sauce in a food processor.
2. Pulse until smooth.
3. Add the coconut milk and mix.
4. Season the chicken with the salt and pepper.
5. Set the Mini Instant Pot to sauté.
6. Add the coconut oil.
7. Cook the onion for 3 minutes.
8. Add the chicken and pour the coconut milk mixture.
9. Cover the pot.
10. Choose manual setting.
11. Cook at high pressure for 15 minutes.
12. Stir in lime juice and garnish with the cilantro leaves before serving.

Nutritional Information per Serving

Calories 135
Total Fat 9.7 g
Saturated Fat 7.7 g
Cholesterol 20 mg
Total Carbs 5.5 g
Sugars 2.3 g
Fiber 1.4 g
Sodium 366 mg
Potassium 195 mg
Protein 7.8 g

SWEET SPICY CHICKEN

Servings: 4
Preparation & Cooking Time: 1 hour and 45 minutes

Ingredients

- 1 lb. chicken thigh (boneless and skinless)
- Salt and pepper to taste
- ½ cup onion, diced
- 2 tsp. garlic, minced
- 2 tbsp. soy sauce
- 1 tbsp. olive oil
- ¼ cup ketchup
- 1 tsp. red pepper flakes
- 1 cup honey
- 2 tbsp. cornstarch
- 1 tbsp. water

Instructions

1. Season the chicken with salt and pepper.
2. In a bowl, mix the onion, garlic, soy sauce, olive oil, ketchup, pepper flakes and honey.
3. Marinate the chicken for 1 hour.
4. Pour the chicken into the Mini Instant Pot.
5. Cover the pot and set it to manual.
6. Cook at high pressure for 25 minutes.
7. Release the pressure naturally.
8. Take 2 tablespoons of the cooking liquid.
9. Combine the cooking liquid, cornstarch and water.
10. Simmer in a saucepan for 2 minutes.
11. Pour the sauce over the chicken before serving.

Nutritional Information per Serving

Calories 546
Total Fat 12.1 g
Saturated Fat 2.8 g
Cholesterol 101 mg
Total Carbs 79.9 g
Sugars 73.8 g
Fiber 0.8 g
Sodium 702 mg
Potassium 430 mg
Protein 34.1 g

CHICKEN WITH FETA & SPINACH

Servings: 2
Preparation & Cooking Time: 30 minutes

Ingredients

- 2 chicken breasts, butterflied
- ¼ cup feta cheese, crumbled
- ¼ cup spinach, chopped
- Salt and pepper to taste
- 1/8 tsp. dried oregano
- 1/8 tsp. dried parsley
- 1/8 tsp. garlic powder
- 1 tbsp. coconut oil
- ½ cup water

Instructions

1. Flatten the chicken with meat mallet.
2. In a bowl, mix the cheese and spinach.
3. Season with the salt and pepper.
4. Divide the mixture and place on top of the chicken breasts.
5. Close the chicken and seal with a butcher's string.
6. Season the outside of the chicken with salt and pepper, oregano, parsley, and garlic powder.
7. Press the sauté function in the Mini Instant Pot.
8. Pour in the coconut oil.
9. Cook the chicken breast until golden brown.
10. Pour the water into the pot.
11. Scrape the bottom part using wooden spoon.
12. Place a steamer rack inside the pot.
13. Put the chicken on top of the rack.
14. Seal the pot.
15. Choose manual.
16. Cook at high pressure for 15 minutes.
17. Release the pressure naturally.

Nutritional Information per Serving

Calories 387
Total Fat 21.6 g
Saturated Fat 11.7 g
Cholesterol 147 mg
Total Carbs 1.1 g
Sugars 0.8 g
Fiber 0.2 g
Sodium 340 mg
Potassium 392 mg
Protein 45.1 g

PESTO CHICKEN

Servings: 2
Preparation & Cooking Time: 50 minutes

Ingredients

- 1 chicken breast, butterflied
- ¼ tsp. dried parsley
- ¼ tsp. garlic powder
- Salt and pepper to taste
- 2 tbsp. coconut oil
- 1 cup water
- ¼ cup ricotta
- ¼ cup pesto
- ¼ cup mozzarella cheese, shredded
- Fresh parsley, chopped

Instructions

1. Season the chicken with the dried parsley, garlic powder, salt and pepper.
2. Pour the coconut oil into the Mini Instant Pot.
3. Cook the chicken for 5 minutes or until golden brown.
4. Transfer the chicken on a plate.
5. Pour the water into the pot.
6. Scrape the bottom using a wooden spoon.
7. Spread the ricotta on top of the chicken.
8. Pour the pesto over the ricotta.
9. Sprinkle shredded mozzarella on top.
10. Wrap the chicken with foil.
11. Place a steamer rack inside the pot.
12. Place the chicken on top of the rack.
13. Close the pot.
14. Choose manual setting.
15. Cook at high pressure for 20 minutes.
16. Release the pressure naturally.
17. Garnish with the parsley before serving.

Nutritional Information per Serving

Calories 363
Total Fat 30.9 g
Saturated Fat 16.2 g
Cholesterol 51 mg
Total Carbs 4 g
Sugars 2.2 g
Fiber 0.6 g
Sodium 279 mg
Potassium 230 mg
Protein 18.2 g

SALMON WITH LEMON & DILL

Servings: 2
Preparation & Cooking Time: 15 minutes

Ingredients

- 2 salmon fillets
- Salt and pepper to taste
- 1 tsp. fresh dill, chopped
- 1 cup water
- 2 tbsp. lemon juice
- 4 lemon slices

Instructions

1. Season the salmon with salt, pepper and dill.
2. Put the steamer rack inside the Mini Instant Pot.
3. Pour the water inside the pot.
4. Put the salmon fillet on top of the steamer rack.
5. Drizzle the lemon juice over the salmon fillets.
6. Place the lemon slices on top.
7. Seal the pot.
8. Choose the steam setting.
9. Cook for 5 minutes.
10. Release the pressure quickly.
11. Garnish with the lemon slices before serving.

Nutritional Information per Serving

Calories 245
Total Fat 11.2 g
Saturated Fat 1.7 g
Cholesterol 78 mg
Total Carbs 1.9 g
Sugars 0.7 g
Fiber 0.5 g
Sodium 86 mg
Potassium 740 mg
Protein 34.9 g

MUSSELS IN GARLIC SAUCE

Servings: 2
Preparation & Cooking Time: 20 minutes

Ingredients

- 4 tbsp. butter
- 4 cloves garlic, minced
- 1 shallot, minced
- 2 lb. mussels, scrubbed, debearded and rinsed
- 1 cup chicken broth
- 1 tbsp. lemon juice
- 3 tbsp. fresh parsley, chopped

Instructions

1. Choose the sauté function in the Mini Instant Pot.
2. Add the butter.
3. Add the garlic and shallot.
4. Cook for 2 minutes.
5. Add the mussels and pour in the broth.
6. Stir in the lemon juice.
7. Seal the pot.
8. Set it to manual.
9. Cook at high pressure for 3 minutes.
10. Release the pressure quickly.
11. Discard mussels that did not open.
12. Pour the liquid over the mussels and garnish with the parsley before serving.

Nutritional Information per Serving

Calories 417
Total Fat 22.7 g
Saturated Fat 11.2 g
Cholesterol 125 mg
Total Carbs 13.1 g
Sugars 0.4 g
Fiber 0.2 g
Sodium 1232 mg
Potassium 1084 mg
Protein 38.2 g

STEAMED FISH WITH MISO BUTTER

Servings: 2
Preparation & Cooking Time: 20 minutes

Ingredients

- 1 cup vegetable broth
- 1 clove garlic, sliced
- 1 ginger, sliced into thin strips
- 2 fish fillets
- Salt and pepper to taste
- 1 tsp. soy sauce
- 1 ½ tsp. miso paste
- 1 tbsp. butter
- 1 tsp. lemon juice

Instructions

1. Pour the broth, garlic and ginger into the Mini Instant Pot.
2. Place the steamer rack inside the pot.
3. Put a foil on top of the rack.
4. Place the fish fillet on top of the foil.
5. Season with the salt, pepper and soy sauce.
6. Seal the pot.
7. Choose manual setting.
8. Cook at low pressure for 10 minutes.
9. Release the pressure quickly.
10. In a bowl, mix the miso paste and butter.
11. Take the fish out of the pot and place on a plate.
12. Drizzle the lemon juice over the fish fillets.
13. Serve the fish with miso butter.

Nutritional Information per Serving

Calories 297
Total Fat 18 g
Saturated Fat 6.5 g
Cholesterol 46 mg
Total Carbs 18.5 g
Sugars 0.8 g
Fiber 0.9 g
Sodium 1217 mg
Potassium 433 mg
Protein 16.7 g

SHRIMP CURRY

Servings: 2
Preparation & Cooking Time: 30 minutes

Ingredients

- 10 shrimp, peeled and deveined
- ½ tsp. chili powder, divided
- 1/4 tsp. turmeric powder, divided
- ½ tsp. garam masala, divided
- Salt to taste
- 1 tbsp. oil
- 2 bay leaves
- 3/4 tsp. cumin seeds
- 1 onion, chopped
- 1 tsp. ginger-garlic paste
- 2 tomatoes, chopped
- 2 tsp. coriander powder
- 1 cup cilantro, chopped
- 3/4 cup water

Instructions

1. In a bowl, mix half of the chili powder, half of the turmeric powder and half of the garam masala.
2. Season the shrimp with this mixture, and with the salt.
3. Set the Mini Instant Pot to sauté.
4. Pour in the oil and cook the bay leaves and cumin seeds.
5. Add the onion and ginger garlic paste.
6. Season with a little salt. Mix well.
7. Add the tomatoes, shrimp, and the remaining spices.
8. Add the water and cilantro.
9. Cook for 5 minutes.
10. Serve warm.

Nutritional Information per Serving

Calories 260
Total Fat 10.8 g
Saturated Fat 1.5 g
Cholesterol 232 mg
Total Carbs 13.5 g
Sugars 5.7 g
Fiber 3.3 g
Sodium 370 mg
Potassium 636 mg
Protein 27.3 g

SALMON IN TERIYAKI SAUCE

Servings: 2
Preparation & Cooking Time: 1 hour

Ingredients

- 1 tbsp. sesame oil
- ¼ cup soy sauce
- ¼ cup mirin
- ¼ cup water
- 1 clove garlic, minced
- 2 tsp. sesame seeds
- 2 tbsp. brown sugar
- 1 tbsp. ginger, grated
- 2 green onions minced
- 2 salmon fillets
- 1 cup water

Instructions

1. In a bowl, mix all the ingredients except the salmon and 1 cup water.
2. Put the salmon on a pan and pour half of the marinade over it.
3. Marinate for 30 minutes.
4. Add 1 cup water into the Mini Instant Pot.
5. Place the steamer rack inside the pot.
6. Seal the pot.
7. Select manual function.
8. Cook at high pressure for 8 minutes.
9. Release the pressure quickly.
10. Take the fish out of the pot.
11. Place it on a serving plate.
12. Press sauté setting in the Mini Instant Pot.
13. Pour the remaining marinade.
14. Simmer until it has thickened.
15. Pour this on top of the fish before serving.

Nutritional Information per Serving

Calories 425
Total Fat 19.5 g
Saturated Fat 2.8 g
Cholesterol 78 mg
Total Carbs 28.4 g
Sugars 17.4 g
Fiber 1 g
Sodium 2140 mg
Potassium 821 mg
Protein 37.4 g

CHAPTER 9: GRACEFUL VEGAN & VEGETARIAN RECIPES (10)

STIR FRIED POTATOES & BELL PEPPER

Servings: 4
Preparation & Cooking Time: 20 minutes

Ingredients

- 1 tbsp. olive oil
- 4 cloves garlic
- 1 potato, sliced into strips
- 2 bell pepper, sliced into strips
- ½ tsp. cumin seeds
- 2 tsp. coriander powder
- ¼ tsp. cayenne powder
- ¼ tsp. turmeric powder
- Salt to taste
- ½ tbsp. lemon juice

Instructions

1. Set the Mini Instant Pot to sauté mode.
2. Add the olive oil.
3. Add the garlic and cook until golden brown.
4. Add the potatoes, bell pepper, cumin seeds, coriander powder, cayenne powder, turmeric powder and salt.
5. Mix well.
6. Cover the pot.
7. Set it to manual.
8. Cook at high pressure for 2 minutes.
9. Release the pressure quickly.
10. Stir in the lemon juice before serving.

Nutritional Information per Serving

Calories 89
Total Fat 3.8 g
Saturated Fat 0.5 g
Cholesterol 0 mg
Total Carbs 13.2 g
Sugars 3.4 g
Fiber 1.9 g
Sodium 44 mg
Potassium 317 mg
Protein 1.7 g

SAVORY BLACK BEANS

Servings: 3
Preparation & Cooking Time: 1 hour and 5 minutes

Ingredients

- 1 tbsp. olive oil
- ½ onion, diced
- 3 cloves garlic, minced
- 1 tsp. chili powder
- 1 ½ tsp. oregano
- ½ tsp. smoked paprika
- ½ tsp. coriander powder
- 2 tsp. cumin
- 1 small bay leaf
- Salt and pepper to taste
- 3 cups vegetable broth
- 1 cup dry black beans, rinsed and drained
- Vegan sour cream
- Fresh cilantro

Instructions

1. Set the Mini Instant Pot to sauté.
2. Pour in the oil.
3. Add the onion, garlic, chili powder, oregano, paprika, coriander powder, cumin, bay leaf, salt and pepper.
4. Cook for 2 minutes, stirring frequently.
5. Pour in the broth and beans.
6. Mix well.
7. Seal the pot.
8. Choose the manual function.
9. Cook at high pressure for 35 minutes.
10. Release the pressure naturally.
11. Serve with sour cream and fresh cilantro.

Nutritional Information per Serving

Calories 425
Total Fat 27 g
Saturated Fat 10.6 g
Cholesterol 65 mg
Total Carbs 19.1 g
Sugars 1.2 g
Fiber 4.2 g
Sodium 1408 mg
Potassium 786 mg
Protein 25.9 g

CAULIFLOWER CURRY

Servings: 4
Preparation & Cooking Time: 25 minutes

Ingredients

- 1 tsp. olive oil
- 1 tsp. cumin seeds
- 1 tsp. mustard seeds
- 1 sprig curry leaf
- 1 red chili
- 1 cup onion, chopped
- 1 tbsp. ginger-garlic paste
- 3 tomatoes, chopped
- 1 tbsp. coriander powder
- 1 tsp. turmeric powder
- 1 ¼ tsp. red chili powder
- 1 tsp. garam masala
- 3 cups cauliflower florets
- 1 cup water
- Salt to taste
- Fresh cilantro leaves

Instructions

1. Choose the sauté mode in the Mini Instant Pot.
2. Pour in the oil.
3. Fry the cumin seeds, mustard seeds, curry leaf and chili.
4. Add the onion and cook for 2 minutes.
5. Add the ginger garlic paste and stir well.
6. Add the tomatoes and cook for 2 minutes.
7. Season with the coriander, turmeric, red chili and garam masala.
8. Add the cauliflower florets.
9. Pour in the water.
10. Season with the salt.
11. Cover the pot.
12. Set it to manual.
13. Cook at high pressure for 3 minutes.
14. Do a quick pressure release.
15. Serve with cilantro.

Nutritional Information per Serving

Calories 185
Total Fat 8.4 g
Saturated Fat 0.5 g
Cholesterol 0 mg
Total Carbs 25.3 g
Sugars 11.2 g
Fiber 8.3 g
Sodium 158 mg
Potassium 1069 mg
Protein 6.5 g

SWEET POTATO CASSEROLE

Servings: 3
Preparation & Cooking Time: 20 minutes

Ingredients

- 1 tbsp. coconut oil
- 1 lb. sweet potatoes
- ¼ tsp. ground cinnamon
- ¼ cup orange juice
- 1/8 tsp. ground nutmeg
- 1/8 cup brown sugar
- Salt to taste
- 10 pecan halves

Instructions

1. Select the sauté function in the Mini Instant Pot.
2. Pour in the coconut oil.
3. Add the sweet potatoes, cinnamon, orange juice and nutmeg. Mix well.
4. Sprinkle the brown sugar on top. Do not mix.
5. Seal the pot.
6. Choose manual.
7. Cook at high pressure for 5 minutes.
8. Release the pressure quickly.
9. Top with the pecans before serving.

Nutritional Information per Serving

Calories 251
Total Fat 4.9 g
Saturated Fat 4 g
Cholesterol 0 mg
Total Carbs 50.4 g
Sugars 8.4 g
Fiber 6.4 g
Sodium 66 mg
Potassium 1284 mg
Protein 2.5 g

COUSCOUS & VEGETABLES

Servings: 4
Preparation & Cooking Time: 25 minutes

Ingredients

- 1 tbsp. olive oil
- 1 onion, chopped
- 2 bay leaves
- 1 cup carrot, grated
- 1 red bell pepper, chopped
- 1 cup couscous
- Salt to taste
- ¼ tsp. garam masala
- 1 cup water
- 1 tbsp. lemon juice

Instructions

1. Press the sauté button in the Mini Instant Pot.
2. Pour in the olive oil.
3. Add the onion and bay leaves.
4. Cook for 2 minutes.
5. Add the carrots and bell pepper.
6. Cook for 1 minute.
7. Add the couscous, garam masala and salt.
8. Pour in the water. Mix well.
9. Cover the pot and set it to manual mode.
10. Cook at high pressure for 2 minutes.
11. Release the pressure naturally.
12. Fluff up the couscous and then stir in the lemon juice before serving.

Nutritional Information per Serving

Calories 225
Total Fat 3.9 g
Saturated Fat 0.6 g
Cholesterol 0 mg
Total Carbs 41.1 g
Sugars 4.1 g
Fiber 3.9 g
Sodium 67 mg
Potassium 261 mg
Protein 6.4 g

LEAFY GREENS WITH GARLIC LEMON SAUCE

Servings: 4
Preparation & Cooking Time: 30 minutes

Ingredients

- 3 cups leafy greens
- ½ cup cashews
- ¼ cup water
- 1 tbsp. lemon juice
- 1 tsp. soy sauce
- Salt to taste
- 1 clove garlic, peeled
- ½ cup water

Instructions

1. Soak the cashews in a cup of water for 10 minutes.
2. After 10 minutes, place the cashews in a blender.
3. Pulse until coarsely chopped.
4. Add the ¼ cup water, lemon juice, soy sauce, salt and garlic.
5. Pulse until smooth.
6. Pour ½ cup water into the Mini Instant Pot.
7. Place a steamer rack inside.
8. Put the greens on top of the rack.
9. Seal the pot.
10. Choose the steam function and set it to 1 minute.
11. Release the pressure quickly.
12. Serve the greens with the lemon garlic sauce.

Nutritional Information per Serving

Calories 112
Total Fat 8 g
Saturated Fat 1.6 g
Cholesterol 0 mg
Total Carbs 7.5 g
Sugars 1.7 g
Fiber 2.1 g
Sodium 193 mg
Potassium 108 mg
Protein 4.3 g

BUTTERED BRUSSELS SPROUTS

Servings: 2
Preparation & Cooking Time: 15 minutes

Ingredients

- 1 cup water
- 2 cups Brussels sprouts, trimmed and sliced
- 1 tbsp. vegan butter
- 1 tbsp. olive oil
- Salt and pepper to taste
- ¼ cup pine nuts, toasted

Instructions

1. Pour the water into the Mini Instant Pot.
2. Add a steamer rack inside the pot.
3. Put the Brussels sprouts on top of the rack.
4. Cover the pot.
5. Choose manual setting.
6. Cook at high pressure for 3 minutes.
7. Release the pressure quickly.
8. Transfer the vegetables to a serving plate.
9. Toss in the butter, olive oil, salt and pepper.
10. Top with the pine nuts before serving.

Nutritional Information per Serving

Calories 213
Total Fat 18.9 g
Saturated Fat 1.9 g
Cholesterol 0 mg
Total Carbs 10.3 g
Sugars 2.5 g
Fiber 3.9 g
Sodium 26 mg
Potassium 445 mg
Protein 5.3 g

BAKED BEANS

Servings: 3
Preparation & Cooking Time: 1 hour and 15 minutes

Ingredients

- 3 cups water
- ½ cup great northern beans, dried
- 1 tsp. olive oil
- 1 onion, chopped
- ¼ cup ketchup
- 1/8 cup brown sugar
- 1/8 cup molasses
- ¼ tsp. garlic powder
- ½ tsp. smoked paprika
- Salt and pepper to taste
- 1 cup water

Instructions

1. Pour 3 cups of water into the Mini Instant Pot.
2. Add the black beans.
3. Cover the pot.
4. Select manual setting.
5. Cook at high pressure for 15 minutes.
6. Release the pressure naturally.
7. Set it to sauté.
8. Pour in the olive oil.
9. Cook the onion for 1 minute.
10. Add the beans.
11. In a bowl, mix the rest of the ingredients.
12. Pour the mixture into the pot.
13. Add 1 cup of water.
14. Choose the manual mode.
15. Cook at high pressure for 40 minutes.
16. Release the pressure naturally.
17. Switch the pot to sauté and simmer until the sauce has thickened.

Nutritional Information per Serving

Calories 215
Total Fat 2.1 g
Saturated Fat 0.4 g
Cholesterol 0 mg
Total Carbs 44 g
Sugars 20.3 g
Fiber 7.2 g
Sodium 235 mg
Potassium 772 mg
Protein 7.5 g

ASPARAGUS & PEAS

Servings: 2
Preparation & Cooking Time: 10 minutes

Ingredients

- 2 cloves garlic, minced
- 2 cups asparagus, sliced
- 1 cup English peas
- ½ cup vegetable broth
- ½ tbsp. lemon juice
- 1 tbsp. lemon zest
- 2 tbsp. almonds, toasted and slivered

Instructions

1. Put the garlic, asparagus and peas in the Mini Instant Pot.
2. Seal the pot.
3. Choose manual mode.
4. Cook at high pressure for 2 minutes.
5. Release the pressure quickly.
6. Stir in the lemon juice and lemon zest.
7. Top with the almonds before serving.

Nutritional Information per Serving

Calories 137
Total Fat 3.8 g
Saturated Fat 0.5 g
Cholesterol 0 mg
Total Carbs 18.9 g
Sugars 7.3 g
Fiber 7.5 g
Sodium 199 mg
Potassium 569 mg
Protein 9.6 g

GARLIC ROSEMARY BABY POTATOES

Servings: 2
Preparation & Cooking Time: 50 minutes

Ingredients

- 2 tbsp. olive oil
- 3 cloves garlic, chopped
- 1 lb. baby potatoes
- 1 sprig rosemary
- 1 cup vegetable stock
- Salt and pepper to taste

Instructions

1. Select the sauté mode in the Mini Instant Pot.
2. Add the olive oil.
3. Add the garlic, potatoes and rosemary.
4. Mix well to coat potatoes with the rosemary.
5. Cook for 10 minutes.
6. Pour the stock into the pot.
7. Cover the pot.
8. Choose manual mode.
9. Cook at high pressure for 11 minutes.
10. Release the pressure quickly.
11. Season with the salt and pepper before serving.

Nutritional Information per Serving

Calories 263
Total Fat 14.4 g
Saturated Fat 2.1 g
Cholesterol 0 mg
Total Carbs 30.6 g
Sugars 0.4 g
Fiber 6.3 g
Sodium 49 mg
Potassium 961 mg
Protein 6.4 g

CHAPTER 10: DELICIOUS SOUP & STEWS RECIPES (10)

BEEF STEW
Servings: 2
Preparation & Cooking Time: 2 hours and 10 minutes

Ingredients
- 1 tbsp. olive oil
- 1 lb. chuck steak
- Salt and pepper to taste
- 1 cup chicken stock
- 1 tbsp. Worcestershire sauce
- 3 tbsp. tomato paste
- 1 tbsp. soy sauce
- 1 tbsp. fish sauce
- 10 mushrooms, sliced thinly
- 2 onions, sliced thinly
- 3 cloves garlic, crushed and minced
- 2 carrots, sliced
- 2 stalks celery, chopped
- ¼ cup sherry wine
- 2 bay leaves
- ¼ tsp. dried thyme
- 3 potatoes, sliced
- ¼ cup peas
- 1 tbsp. flour

Instructions
1. Season the steak with salt and pepper.

2. Press sauté in the Mini Instant Pot.
3. Pour in the oil.
4. Brown the steak for 6 minutes per side.
5. Remove from the pot and set aside.
6. In a bowl, mix the chicken stock, Worcestershire sauce, soy sauce, fish sauce and tomato paste. Set aside.
7. Add the mushrooms to the pot.
8. Cook until brown.
9. Remove the mushrooms from the pot and set aside.
10. Add a little more oil to the pot.
11. Cook the onion and garlic for 1 minute.
12. Add the celery and carrots.
13. Season with salt and pepper.
14. Deglaze the pot with the sherry wine.
15. Scrape the bottom of the pot with a wooden spoon.
16. Add the bay leaves, thyme, potatoes and chicken stock mixture.
17. Close the pot.
18. Choose manual setting.
19. Cook at high pressure for 4 minutes.
20. Release the pressure quickly.
21. Slice the beef into cubes.
22. Add the beef along with its juice in a bowl and stir in the flour.
23. Open the pot. Remove the vegetables and set aside.
24. Put the beef with the thickened sauce.
25. Close the pot.
26. Cook at high pressure for 32 minutes.
27. Release the pressure naturally.
28. Uncover the pot.
29. Put the vegetables back inside.
30. Top with the sautéed mushrooms before serving.

Nutritional Information per Serving
Calories 520
Total Fat 19 g
Saturated Fat 6.4 g
Cholesterol 120 mg
Total Carbs 42.6 g
Sugars 9.8 g
Fiber 7.5 g
Sodium 941 mg
Potassium 1487 mg
Protein 42.3 g

MINESTRONE SOUP

Servings: 4
Preparation & Cooking Time: 40 minutes

Ingredients

- ½ cup olive oil
- ½ lb. bacon
- 1 onion, diced
- 5 cloves garlic, crushed and minced
- 3 stalks celery, diced
- 1 carrot, diced
- 8 cups bone broth
- 1 potato, diced
- 1 zucchini, diced
- 2 cups cabbage, chopped
- 2 cups tomato sauce
- 2 tbsp. fresh sage, chopped
- 1 tbsp. dried oregano
- 2 tbsp. nutritional yeast
- Salt to taste
- ¼ cup parsley, chopped
- 8 oz. spinach, chopped

Instructions

1. Set the Mini Instant Pot to sauté.
2. Pour in the olive oil.
3. Cook the bacon until golden crispy.
4. Add the onion, garlic, celery and carrot.
5. Cook for 2 minutes, stirring occasionally.
6. Pour in the broth.
7. Add the rest of the ingredients except the parsley and spinach.
8. Cover the pot.
9. Choose the soup setting.
10. Cook for 20 minutes.
11. Release the pressure naturally.
12. Stir in the parsley and spinach before serving in bowls.

Nutritional Information per Serving

Calories 665
Total Fat 50.1 g
Saturated Fat 11.7 g
Cholesterol 62 mg
Total Carbs 30.1 g
Sugars 10 g
Fiber 9 g
Sodium 2077 mg
Potassium 1716 mg
Protein 29.5 g

CILANTRO & LEMON SOUP

Servings: 4
Preparation & Cooking Time: 30 minutes

Ingredients

- 1 cup cilantro
- 2 tsp. cumin seeds
- 4 cloves garlic, minced
- 1 ½ tbsp. ginger, grated
- 2 green chili
- Pepper to taste
- 1 tbsp. olive oil
- ½ tsp. mustard seeds
- ½ tsp. turmeric powder
- 1 sprig curry leaves
- ½ tsp. yellow lentils
- Salt to taste
- Water
- 1 tbsp. lemon juice

Instructions

1. Put the cilantro, cumin seeds, garlic, ginger, chili and pepper in a food processor.
2. Pulse until the mixture turns into paste.
3. Set aside.
4. Choose the sauté setting in the Mini Instant Pot.
5. Add the olive oil.
6. Add the mustard seeds, turmeric and curry leaves.
7. Cook for 1 minute.
8. Add the cilantro paste.
9. Mix and cook for 2 minutes.
10. Add the yellow lentils.
11. Season with the salt.
12. Add water, depending on the consistency you prefer.
13. Cover the pot.
14. Choose manual.
15. Cook at high pressure for 8 minutes.
16. Release the pressure naturally.
17. Add more water if you like.
18. Stir in the lemon juice before serving.

Nutritional Information per Serving

Calories 111
Total Fat 7.9 g
Saturated Fat 1.1 g
Cholesterol 0 mg
Total Carbs 9.8 g
Sugars 5.2 g
Fiber 0.9 g
Sodium 208 mg
Potassium 133 mg
Protein 1.2 g

CARROT SOUP

Servings: 4
Preparation & Cooking Time: 20 minutes

Ingredients

- 1 tbsp. olive oil
- 1 onion, diced
- 1 clove garlic, crushed and minced
- 8 carrots, sliced into cubes
- 15 oz. coconut milk
- 2 cups vegetable broth
- Salt and pepper to taste
- Chopped parsley
- Coconut cream

Instructions

1. Press the sauté button in the Mini Instant Pot.
2. Pour in the olive oil.
3. Cook the onion and garlic for 2 minutes.
4. Add the carrots.
5. Pour in the coconut milk.
6. Season with the salt and pepper.
7. Cover the pot.
8. Choose manual mode.
9. Cook at high pressure for 8 minutes.
10. Release the pressure naturally.
11. Pour the contents into a blender.
12. Pulse until smooth.
13. Serve with parsley and coconut cream.

Nutritional Information per Serving

Calories 356
Total Fat 29.6 g
Saturated Fat 23.2 g
Cholesterol 0 mg
Total Carbs 21.2 g
Sugars 11.1 g
Fiber 6 g
Sodium 483 mg
Potassium 816 mg
Protein 6.2 g

BROCCOLI CHEDDAR SOUP

Servings: 4
Preparation & Cooking Time: 30 minutes

Ingredients

- ¼ cup olive oil
- 1 onion, chopped
- 4 cloves garlic, minced
- 1 lb. broccoli, chopped
- 3 cups chicken broth
- 1 cup milk
- 1 tbsp. ginger, grated
- Salt and pepper to taste
- 1 ½ cups cheddar cheese, grated

Instructions

1. Set the Mini Instant Pot to sauté.
2. Pour in the olive oil.
3. Add the onion and garlic.
4. Cook for 2 minutes.
5. Add the broccoli, chicken broth, milk, ginger, salt and pepper.
6. Cover the pot.
7. Select manual function.
8. Cook at high pressure for 5 minutes.
9. Release the pressure naturally.
10. Puree using an immersion blender.
11. Stir in the cheddar cheese before serving.

Nutritional Information per Serving

Calories 397
Total Fat 29.4 g
Saturated Fat 11.8 g
Cholesterol 50 mg
Total Carbs 16.3 g
Sugars 6.7 g
Fiber 3.8 g
Sodium 904 mg
Potassium 661 mg
Protein 20 g

BUTTERNUT SQUASH SOUP

Servings: 3
Preparation & Cooking Time: 30 minutes

Ingredients

- 1 tbsp. olive oil
- ½ onion, chopped
- 1 sprig sage
- Salt and pepper to taste
- 2 lb. butternut squash, sliced into cubes
- 2 cups vegetable stock
- 1 tsp. ginger, minced
- 1/8 tsp. nutmeg
- ½ cup pumpkin seeds, toasted

Instructions

1. Select the sauté mode in the Mini Instant Pot.
2. Pour olive oil.
3. Add the onion, sage, salt and pepper.
4. Cook for 1 minute.
5. Push the onion on one side.
6. Add the squash cubes.
7. Cook for 10 minutes.
8. Pour in the stock.
9. Stir in the ginger and nutmeg.
10. Close the pot.
11. Choose manual setting.
12. Cook at high pressure for 15 minutes.
13. Release the pressure naturally.
14. Discard the sage stem.
15. Transfer the contents to a blender.
16. Puree until smooth.
17. Garnish with the pumpkin seeds before serving.

Nutritional Information per Serving

Calories 311
Total Fat 15.6 g
Saturated Fat 2.8 g
Cholesterol 0 mg
Total Carbs 41.7 g
Sugars 7.8 g
Fiber 7.5 g
Sodium 21 mg
Potassium 1286 mg
Protein 9 g

CLAM CHOWDER

Servings: 2
Preparation & Cooking Time: 30 minutes

Ingredients

- ½ cup bacon, cubed
- 1 onion, chopped
- Salt and pepper to taste
- ¼ cup white wine
- 1 potato, cubed
- 1 cup clam juice
- 1 sprig thyme
- 1 bay leaf
- ¼ tsp. cayenne pepper
- 5 oz. fresh clams, scrubbed, rinsed and drained
- ½ cup milk
- ½ cup cream
- ½ tbsp. butter
- ½ tbsp. flour

Instructions

1. Set the Mini Instant Pot to sauté.
2. Cook the bacon until golden crispy.
3. Add the onion, salt and pepper.
4. Deglaze by pouring in the wine.
5. Scrape the brown bits using a wooden spoon.
6. Simmer until wine has been reduced.
7. Add the potatoes and clam juice.
8. Add the thyme, bay leaf and cayenne pepper.
9. Close the pot.
10. Choose manual mode.
11. Cook at high pressure for 5 minutes.
12. Release the pressure naturally.
13. In a small bowl, mix the butter and flour.
14. Stir in the butter mixture into the spoon.
15. Add the clam meat, cream and milk.
16. Simmer in sauté setting for 5 to 8 minutes.

Nutritional Information per Serving

Calories 351
Total Fat 15.7 g
Saturated Fat 7.3 g
Cholesterol 45 mg
Total Carbs 35.3 g
Sugars 9.6 g
Fiber 3.5 g
Sodium 773 mg
Potassium 703 mg
Protein 12.6 g

CORN & ZUCCHINI CHOWDER WITH BACON BITS

Servings: 4
Preparation & Cooking Time: 40 minutes

Ingredients

- 1 tbsp. olive oil
- 2 zucchinis, sliced
- 1 tsp. thyme
- 2 green onions, chopped
- Salt and pepper to taste
- ½ lb. bacon, diced
- 1 onion, diced
- 2 cloves garlic, minced
- 2 potatoes, diced
- 1 cup corn kernels
- 1 bay leaf
- 2 ½ cups water
- 1 cup heavy cream
- 1 cup milk

Instructions

1. Set the Mini Instant Pot to sauté.
2. Add the olive oil.
3. Cook the zucchini, thyme and green onion for 5 minutes.
4. Season with the salt and pepper.
5. Transfer to a bowl and set aside.
6. Add the bacon and cook for 5 minutes.
7. Transfer to a plate.
8. Add the onion and cook for 3 minutes.
9. Add the garlic and cook for 30 seconds.
10. Add the potatoes, corn kernels, half of the bacon, bay leaf and water.
11. Season with the salt and pepper.
12. Seal the pot.
13. Choose manual function.
14. Cook at high pressure for 5 minutes.
15. Release the pressure naturally.
16. Stir in the rest of the ingredients and top with the remaining bacon before serving.

Nutritional Information per Serving

Calories 609
Total Fat 40.4 g
Saturated Fat 16.1 g
Cholesterol 108 mg
Total Carbs 35.7 g
Sugars 8.3 g
Fiber 5.6 g
Sodium 1379 mg
Potassium 1243 mg
Protein 28.4 g

FRENCH ONION, BEEF & MUSHROOM STEW

Servings: 4
Preparation & Cooking Time: 5 hours and 30 minutes

Ingredients

- 1 tbsp. olive oil
- 10 oz. cremini mushrooms, divided
- Salt and pepper to taste
- 2 tbsp. butter
- 2 onion, sliced thinly
- 2 tbsp. flour
- 1 ½ cup dry white wine
- 1lb. beef stew meat, sliced into cubes
- 4 cups beef broth
- 5 sprigs thyme
- 2 oz. Gruyere cheese, grated

Instructions

1. Choose the sauté mode in the Mini Instant Pot.
2. Add the olive oil.
3. Cook the mushrooms for 8 minutes and season with the salt and pepper.
4. Transfer the mushrooms to a plate.
5. Add the butter and cook the onions for 10 minutes.
6. Sprinkle the flour all over the onions.
7. Stir for 1 minute.
8. Add the wine and simmer until reduced by half.
9. Add the beef, broth and thyme.
10. Cover the pot.
11. Choose the slow cook setting.
12. Cook for 5 hours.
13. Release the pressure quickly.
14. Discard the sprigs and stir in the cheese before serving.

Nutritional Information per Serving

Calories 521
Total Fat 22.5 g
Saturated Fat 9.9 g
Cholesterol 132 mg
Total Carbs 15.2 g
Sugars 5 g
Fiber 2.2 g
Sodium 938 mg
Potassium 1176 mg
Protein 46.5 g

KALE & POTATO SOUP

Servings: 3
Preparation & Cooking Time: 30 minutes

Ingredients

- 1 tbsp. olive oil
- 1 cup leeks, trimmed
- 1 lb. potato, sliced into cubes
- 1 clove garlic, minced
- 3 cups vegetable broth
- 4 oz. kale leaves, chopped
- ¼ tsp. apple cider vinegar
- Salt and pepper to taste
- Chopped green onion

Instructions

1. Choose the sauté mode in the Mini Instant Pot.
2. Add the oil and cook the leeks for 8 minutes.
3. Add the potatoes, garlic and broth.
4. Cover the pot.
5. Choose manual setting.
6. Cook at high pressure for 6 minutes.
7. Release the pressure quickly.
8. Mash the potatoes.
9. Stir in the kale.
10. Cover the pot.
11. Cook at high pressure for 2 minutes.
12. Release the pressure quickly.
13. Stir in the vinegar, season with the salt and garnish with the green onion before serving.

Nutritional Information per Serving

Calories 235
Total Fat 6.3 g
Saturated Fat 1.1 g
Cholesterol 0 mg
Total Carbs 36.2 g
Sugars 3.2 g
Fiber 4.6 g
Sodium 796 mg
Potassium 1100 mg
Protein 9.6 g

CHAPTER 11: GREAT APPETIZERS & SNACKS RECIPES (5)

CHEESE POPCORN

Servings: 2
Preparation & Cooking Time: 15 minutes

Ingredients
- 1 tbsp. unsalted butter
- 2 tbsp. coconut oil
- ½ cup corn kernels
- 1 tbsp. cheese powder

Instructions
1. Click the sauté button in the Mini Instant Pot.
2. Add the butter and coconut oil.
3. Mix well.
4. Add the corn kernels.
5. Cook for 1 minute.

6. Close the pot.
7. Wait for the popping to finish.
8. Toss the popcorn in cheese powder before serving.

Nutritional Information per Serving

Calories 201
Total Fat 19.8 g
Saturated Fat 15.5 g
Cholesterol 15 mg
Total Carbs 7.3 g
Sugars 1.3 g
Fiber 1.1 g
Sodium 47 mg
Potassium 106 mg
Protein 1.3 g

CHICKEN LIVER PATE' SPREAD & CRACKERS

Servings: 6
Preparation & Cooking Time: 15 minutes

Ingredients

- 1 tsp. olive oil
- 1 onion, chopped
- Salt and pepper to taste
- ¾ lb. chicken liver
- 1 bay leaf
- ¼ cup red wine
- 1 tbsp. capers
- 2 anchovies in oil
- 1 tbsp. butter
- 1 tsp. rum
- Whole grain crackers

Instructions

1. Pour the olive oil in the Mini Instant Pot.
2. Press the sauté function.
3. Add the onion, salt and pepper.
4. Cook for 1 minute.
5. Add the chicken liver and bay leaf.
6. Sear for 2 minutes.
7. Deglaze with the red wine.
8. Scrape the brown bits using a wooden spoon.
9. Close the pot.
10. Choose manual mode.
11. Cook at high pressure for 5 minutes.
12. Release the pressure naturally.
13. Discard the bay leaf.
14. Add the capers and anchovies.
15. Transfer to a blender.
16. Pulse until smooth.
17. Stir in the butter and rum.
18. Serve with whole grain crackers.

Nutritional Information per Serving

Calories 136
Total Fat 6.4 g
Saturated Fat 2.5 g
Cholesterol 324 mg
Total Carbs 2.6 g
Sugars 0.9 g
Fiber 0.5 g
Sodium 100 mg
Potassium 187 mg
Protein 14.1 g

DUMPLINGS

Servings: 3
Preparation & Cooking Time: 30 minutes

Ingredients

- ¼ lb. ground pork
- ¼ lb. shrimp, peeled and chopped
- ¼ tsp. oil
- ½ tsp. sesame oil
- 1 tbsp. chicken stock
- 1 tsp. cornstarch
- 1 tsp. soy sauce
- ½ tsp. fish sauce
- ¼ tsp. sugar
- 1 slice ginger, grated
- ½ stalk green onion, chopped
- Salt and white pepper to taste
- 10 wonton wrappers
- 2 cups water

Instructions

1. In a bowl, combine all the ingredients except the wonton wrapper and water.
2. Mix well.
3. Scoop a tablespoon of the mixture on top of each wonton wrapper.
4. Wrap and seal.
5. Place a steamer rack inside the Mini Instant Pot.
6. Pour the water into the pot.
7. Add the dumplings on top of the rack.
8. Cover the pot.
9. Set it to manual.
10. Cook at high pressure for 3 minutes.
11. Let it sit for 5 minutes.
12. Release the pressure quickly.
13. Cook another batch if there are any uncooked dumplings left.

Nutritional Information per Serving

Calories 428
Total Fat 4.8 g
Saturated Fat 1.1 g
Cholesterol 117 mg
Total Carbs 64.1 g
Sugars 0.4 g
Fiber 2 g
Sodium 917 mg
Potassium 326 mg
Protein 29.2 g

GARLIC & HONEY CHICKEN WINGS

Servings: 4
Preparation & Cooking Time: 50 minutes

Ingredients

- 1 tsp. sugar
- 2 tbsp. soy sauce
- Salt to taste
- 1 lb. chicken wings
- 1 tbsp. peanut oil
- ½ shallot, minced
- 4 cloves garlic, minced
- 1 tbsp. ginger, grated
- 1 tbsp. honey
- ½ cup water

Instructions

1. Mix the sugar, soy sauce and salt in a bowl.
2. Soak the chicken wings in this mixture for 20 minutes.
3. Set the Mini Instant Pot to sauté.
4. Add the oil.
5. Put the chicken inside the pot.
6. Cook for 1 minute or until brown.
7. Set aside.
8. Add the shallot, garlic and ginger.
9. Cook for 1 minute.
10. Mix the honey and water and add to the pot.
11. Put the chicken back and stir to coat evenly.
12. Close the pot.
13. Set it to manual.
14. Cook at high pressure for 5 minutes.
15. Release the pressure naturally.

Nutritional Information per Serving

Calories 278
Total Fat 11.9 g
Saturated Fat 2.9 g
Cholesterol 101 mg
Total Carbs 7.9 g
Sugars 5.5 g
Fiber 0.3 g
Sodium 588 mg
Potassium 326 mg
Protein 33.6 g

CAJUN TRAIL MIX

Servings: 5 to 10
Preparation & Cooking Time: 30 minutes

Ingredients

- 1 cup chickpeas, drained
- 1 cup raw pecan halves
- ½ cup raw almonds
- ½ cup cashews
- ¼ cup sunflower seeds
- 2 tbsp. butter
- 1 tbsp. water
- ¼ cup maple syrup
- ½ tbsp. Cajun seasoning mix
- Salt to taste

Instructions

1. Mix all the ingredients in the Mini Instant Pot.
2. Press the sauté button.
3. Cook until a little sticky.
4. Cover the pot.
5. Choose manual mode.
6. Cook at high pressure for 10 minutes.
7. Release the pressure quickly.
8. Spread the mixture on a baking sheet.
9. Bake in the oven at 375 degrees F for 7 minutes.
10. Let cool before serving.

Nutritional Information per Serving

Calories 407
Total Fat 28.1 g
Saturated Fat 4.9 g
Cholesterol 9 mg
Total Carbs 32.7 g
Sugars 11.3 g
Fiber 8.4 g
Sodium 56 mg
Potassium 472 mg
Protein 11 g

CHEESECAKE BITES

Servings: 4
Preparation & Cooking Time: 30 minutes

Ingredients

- 8 oz. cream cheese
- ½ cup powdered sugar
- ¼ cup flour
- 1 tsp. vanilla extract
- 1/8 cup sour cream
- 1 egg, beaten
- 1 cup water

Instructions

1. In a bowl, mix the cream cheese and sugar.
2. Slowly add the flour, vanilla and sour cream.
3. Fold in the egg. Mix well.
4. Pour the batter into silicone molds.

5. Cover the molds with foil.
6. Pour the water into the Mini Instant Pot.
7. Add a steamer rack inside.
8. Put the molds on top of the rack.
9. Cover the pot.
10. Choose manual setting.
11. Cook at low pressure for 15 minutes.
12. Release the pressure naturally.
13. Let cool or chill in the refrigerator before serving.

Nutritional Information per Serving
Calories 319
Total Fat 22.5 g
Saturated Fat 13.7 g
Cholesterol 106 mg
Total Carbs 22.9 g
Sugars 15 g
Fiber 0.2 g
Sodium 189 mg
Potassium 103 mg
Protein 6.7 g

MANGO WITH SWEETENED RICE

Servings: 3
Preparation & Cooking Time: 30 minutes

Ingredients

- ½ cup white rice, rinsed and drained
- ¼ cup sugar
- Salt to taste
- 3 cups milk
- 1 egg, beaten
- ½ tsp. vanilla extract
- ½ cup mango cubes
- 1 tbsp. honey

Instructions

1. Mix the rice, sugar, salt and milk in the Mini Instant Pot.
2. Seal the pot.
3. Choose manual mode.
4. Cook at high pressure for 10 minutes.
5. Release the pressure naturally.
6. Slowly whisk in the egg to the rice mixture.
7. Turn on the sauté function.
8. Simmer for 3 minutes.
9. Stir in the vanilla extract and mango cubes.
10. Drizzle honey on top before serving.

Nutritional Information per Serving

Calories 337
Total Fat 6.8 g
Saturated Fat 3.5 g
Cholesterol 75 mg
Total Carbs 57.6 g
Sugars 31.7 g
Fiber 0.8 g
Sodium 188 mg
Potassium 243 mg
Protein 12.3 g

PEACH COBBLER

Servings: 2
Preparation & Cooking Time: 40 minutes

Ingredients

- 3 cups peaches, chopped
- 1 cup sugar
- 1 tbsp. flour

- 1 tbsp. corn starch
- ½ tsp. lemon juice
- ½ cup water

For the toppings:

- 1 cup flour
- ½ cup sugar
- 1 tsp. baking powder

- ½ tsp. salt
- 4 tbsp. butter
- ½ cup buttermilk

Instructions

1. Place the peaches, 1 cup sugar, 1 tablespoon flour, corn starch and lemon juice in a large bowl. Mix well.
2. Pour the water into the Mini Instant Pot.
3. Choose the sauté setting.
4. Let the water boil before adding the peaches.
5. In another bowl, mix the rest of the ingredients.
6. Pour this mixture over the peaches.
7. Close the pot.
8. Select manual mode.
9. Cook at high pressure for 20 minutes.
10. Release the pressure naturally.
11. Serve with vanilla ice cream.

Nutritional Information per Serving

Calories 725
Total Fat 24.2 g
Saturated Fat 15 g
Cholesterol 64 mg
Total Carbs 132 g
Sugars 124 g
Fiber 3.6 g
Sodium 814 mg
Potassium 786 mg
Protein 4.8 g

SWEETENED COCONUT RICE

Servings: 3
Preparation & Cooking Time: 45 minutes

Ingredients

- ½ cup rice, rinsed
- ½ tsp. saffron
- ½ tbsp. milk
- 1 tbsp. coconut oil
- 10 cashews
- 3 cloves
- 1 cardamom pod
- 1 cup water
- ¼ tsp. salt
- ½ cup coconut flakes
- ½ cup sugar
- 1 tbsp. raisins
- ½ tsp. cardamom powder

Instructions

1. Soak the rice in water for 20 minutes.
2. Drain the rice, set aside.
3. Soak the saffron in milk and set aside.
4. Set the Mini Instant Pot to sauté.
5. Add the coconut oil.
6. Cook the cashews until brown.
7. Remove from the pot and set aside.
8. Add the cloves and cardamom to the pot.
9. Cook for 10 seconds.
10. Add the rice.
11. Stir for 1 minute.
12. Pour in the water.
13. Mix well.
14. Seal the pot.
15. Choose manual.
16. Cook at high pressure for 6 minutes.
17. Release the pressure naturally.
18. Stir in the rest of the ingredients.
19. Press the sauté setting.
20. Cook for 5 minutes.
21. Garnish with the cashews and saffron.

Nutritional Information per Serving

Calories 597
Total Fat 30.4 g
Saturated Fat 12.1 g
Cholesterol 0 mg
Total Carbs 77.5 g

Sugars 38.4 g
Fiber 3.1 g
Sodium 207 mg
Potassium 367 mg
Protein 9.8 g

STEWED PEARS

Servings: 2
Preparation & Cooking Time: 15 minutes

Ingredients

- 2 cups red wine
- 2 pears, peeled but with stem still attached
- 1 bay leaf
- ¼ tsp. cinnamon
- ¼ tsp. ginger
- ½ cup sugar
- 1 tsp. oregano

Instructions

1. Pour the red wine into the Mini Instant Pot.
2. Add all the ingredients. Mix well.
3. Cover the pot.
4. Choose manual setting.
5. Cook at high pressure for 7 minutes.
6. Release the pressure naturally.
7. Take the pears out.
8. Press the sauté button and simmer the sauce until reduced to half.
9. Pour the sauce over the pears and serve.

Nutritional Information per Serving

Calories 508
Total Fat 0.4 g
Saturated Fat 0 g
Cholesterol 0 mg
Total Carbs 89.1 g
Sugars 72 g
Fiber 7 g
Sodium 15 mg
Potassium 493 mg
Protein 1 g

CONCLUSION

With the help of the Mini Instant Pot, you can finally say goodbye to the health perils of fast food and instant food products.

You can start living a healthier life by making your own healthy and delicious dishes that won't require you to spend long hours in the kitchen.

For sure, you're going to find this versatile kitchen device a good cooking ally.

Have fun!

APPENDIX: MEASUREMENT CONVERSION TABLE

Unit	Conversion	Conversion
1 teaspoon	1/3 tablespoon	1/6 ounce
1 tablespoon	3 teaspoons	½ ounce
1/8 cup	2 tablespoons	1 ounce
¼ cup	4 tablespoons	2 ounces
1/3 cup	¼ cup and 4 teaspoons	2 ¾ ounces
½ cup	8 tablespoons	4 ounces
1 cup	½ pint	8 ounces
1 pint	2 cups	16 ounces
1 quart	4 cups	32 ounces
1 liter	1 quart and ¼ cup	4 ¼ cups
1 gallon	4 quarts	16 cups

Made in the USA
Middletown, DE
30 November 2018